DENIS MCBRIDE

JESUS
& the Gospels

a redemptorist publication

BY THE SAME AUTHOR

The Gospel of Luke: a Reflective Commentary
Emmaus: the Gracious Visit of God According to Luke
Seasons of the Word: Reflections on the Sunday Readings
Impressions of Jesus
The Gospel of Mark: a Reflective Commentary
The Parables of Jesus

(all available from Redemptorist Publications)

Published by Redemptorist Publications
Alphonsus House Chawton Hampshire GU34 3HQ England

Copyright © Denis McBride
Editor: Rosemary Gallagher

First Printing: May 2002

ISBN: 085231 258 X

Design: Orchid Design

Printed by: Polar Group

CONTENTS

The essentials of the Jesus story and how the four evangelists variously present the major moments in their narratives

		PAGE
	Preface	7
	Introduction: The Bible: the living word of God	9
1	First images of Jesus	14
2	Uncovering the original relationship	21
3	Fascination and discipleship: a reflection	27
4	Beginning with the passion and death	34
5	The passion	38
6	Language and the passion	48
7	The resurrection	51
8	Emmaus: broken discipleship renewed	56
9	The ascension of Jesus	59
10	Establishing an apostolic community of memory and spirit	60
11	Recognising Paul's contribution	64
12	How the Gospels developed backwards	68
13	The development of early Christology	72
14	Bringing the past up to date	74
15	The infancy narratives	78
16	The structure of Luke's infancy narrative	83

CONTENTS cont.

17   Luke's infancy narrative: three notes   85

18   John the Baptist and Jesus in the Gospels   86

     Political Map   94

     Geographical Map   95

19   The baptism of Jesus   96

20   John's influence on Jesus   98

21   The temptations of Jesus   103

22   The kingdom of God   106

23   The parables and the kingdom   110

24   The miracles of Jesus   114

25   Jesus and table fellowship   118

26   At the table of Simon the Pharisee   126

27   The transfiguration   130

28   Suffering, prayer and passion   135

29   In memory of him: retelling the stories of Jesus   138

PREFACE

A confession, to begin: this book is radically incomplete. This is not a pious thought or, indeed, theological humility in the face of such a comprehensive topic; it is a simple observation. These pages make up the outline notes for one of the courses I offer, *Jesus and the Gospels*, and, I hope, they will continue to serve this purpose. This programme of reflection, or some of it, has been offered to a variety of groups in a variety of places:

✳ The Redemptorist pastoral centres in the UK: Hawkstone Hall, Shropshire, and St Mary's, Perth; ✳ The Institute of St Anselm, Kent; ✳ St Patrick's College, Maynooth, Ireland; ✳ The Conference of Irish Bishops; ✳ The Catholic Teachers of Sarawak, East Malaysia; ✳ The Dei Verbum and Priests' Renewal Programme in Nemi, Rome; ✳ Gaba Pastoral Centre, Kenya; ✳ Sampran Pastoral Centre, Bangkok; ✳ The Maryhill School of Theology, Manila; ✳ St Louis University, Philippines; ✳ Catholic Pastoral Centre, Sibu, Borneo; ✳ Manresa Jesuit Centre, Toronto; ✳ The SVD missionaries and Holy Spirit Sisters, Botswana; ✳ The Assumptionist Sisters, Tokyo.

Coming from a wee town in Scotland, it has been a wonderful privilege to travel to unpronounceable places and meet such a wide variety of peoples and cultures, my ticket being to talk about Jesus and the Gospels. Many students have encouraged me to publish the notes in book form, in the hope that they may reach a wider audience and might stand on their own as a resource for students of the Gospel. In that hope Rosemary Gallagher, the editorial director of Redemptorist Publications, has kindly agreed to publish this book.

I have included a number of religious paintings and modern poems to enliven the text and provide other ways of reflecting on the Jesus story and our own. I hope that the written material in these pages may make sense, independent of the lectures, as reflective markers in the study of the Gospels. Only you, dear reader, can judge if that hope is more than a fragile one.

Denis McBride CSSR
Hawkstone Hall

INTRODUCTION

The Bible: The Living Word of God

1 The Bible is one of the principal treasures of the Church because it contains the human expression of divine revelation, the disclosure of the word of God within the human story. As God's word the Bible has both the divine element ("God's") and the human element ("word"), and this dramatic interplay between the divine and the human is explored throughout its pages. The English word "Bible" is derived from the Greek word *biblia*, which simply means "books" – referring to the authoritative collection of Jewish and Christian texts.

2 No single human being planned the Bible. The Bible has gradually emerged over countless generations as a collection of books, a sacred library, which celebrates two intertwining stories: God's search for the heart of humankind and our human search for God. The series of books, inspired and inspiring, contains a variety of privileged experiences of God and different ways of celebrating those moments. The Christian Bible is divided into two distinct parts. The first part is the Hebrew Bible or the Old Testament, which celebrates the story of God's dealings with the people of Israel. The second part is the New Testament, which celebrates God's new outreach to humanity through the person of Jesus, his Son (see Heb 1:1-2).

3 In the Hebrew Bible the word of God is always concerned with a people and its history – the word calls the people, it awakens their sense of God and goodness, and seeks to shape the story of their lives. When we read the ancient books we are drawn into the living drama of God's revelation and how different generations manage their response. We witness how people convert their experience into story and offer it to others as a gift of life. They share their memories and dreams, their anguish and hopes; they commit to writing their sacred laws and customs; they retell ancient epics of heroism and failure; they preserve their history, the wise sayings of the prophets and the poetry of the sages. Through all the collected writings the authors constantly speak of God's enduring love while at the same time chronicling the people's fitful responses.

4 Among the twenty-seven books of the New Testament special place is given to the four Gospels, which celebrate the memory of Jesus and focus on his death and resurrection as the defining moments of his unique story. While Jesus himself centred his Gospel preaching on the kingdom of God, the early apostolic preachers, through the prompting of the Spirit, changed the focal point of the preached Gospel to the person of Jesus himself, concentrating on his death and resurrection. Thus Saint Paul, writing to the Christian community at Corinth about AD 57, gives a summary of the early apostolic Gospel that he delivered as he himself had received it: that Christ died, that he was buried, that he was raised to life on the third day, and that he appeared to a number of witnesses (1 Cor 15:1-8). By the time the evangelists come to write their versions of the Gospel, however, they have the task the early preachers did not: they have to provide a narrative sequence to the preached Jesus tradition.[1]

---

1. See *Instruction Concerning the Historical Truth of the Gospels* (Pontifical Biblical Commission, 1964) n.IX.

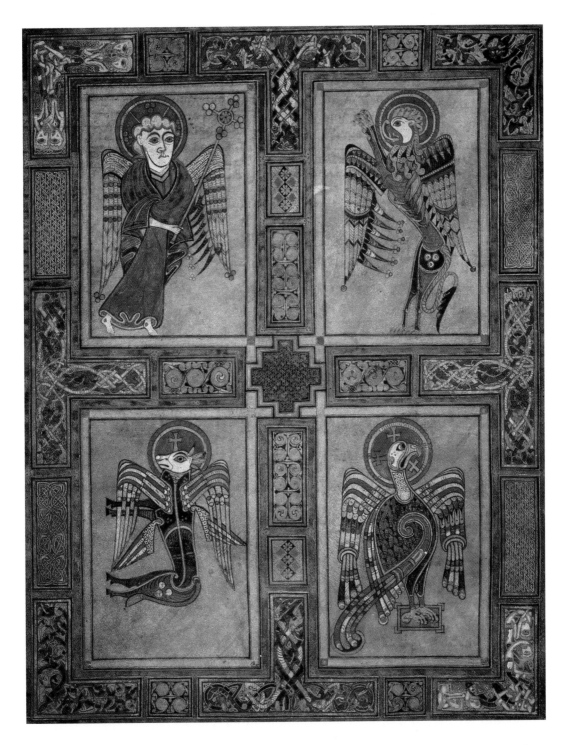

The Four Evangelists:
(Book of Kells, Folio 27v)

5   It is the Church that gives birth to the Gospels, not vice versa. The whole of the New Testament writing emerges from different Christian communities that seek to spread the liberating message of Jesus and confirm existing believers in their faith. In so doing, they constantly refer back to the Hebrew Bible as a rich source for the new story they are writing (cf. Lk 24:44; Jn 5:39). From the second century onwards, the two Testaments are seen as the seamless story of God's revelation: the God who liberated his chosen people from bondage in Egypt is the same God who liberates a broken and sinful humanity in the death and resurrection of Jesus.

6   The Bible is not written in code for a select few; rather, it is offered to the whole of humanity as a living voice to guide us on our journey to God and in our dealings with one another. Certainly it has to be admitted that among the writings there are lists and genealogies and purification rubrics that remind us of discarded telephone directories: they evoke no response and lead to little insight. But there are passages of matchless beauty that call out to us from a culture and time different from ours to the heart of our own experience. The great narrative thrust of the Bible is a call from a world of conflict and suffering and passion to our own world of conflict and suffering and passion; it bids us not to limit wisdom to our own generation but to learn about God and grow wise about one another from the shared insight of those who have journeyed before us. For all our real differences from our ancestors in the faith, we are not total strangers, but fellow pilgrims journeying towards our common destiny in God.

7   The whole Bible provides us with a vast moving picture in which our own stories can find new meaning. Our own life stories are illuminated when seen within the larger frame of the biblical narrative. We meet people at the crossroads of life: a father, without argument and without tears, walks with his son on a silent journey towards holocaust; a refugee people, tormented by years of abuse, find an unlikely liberator in Moses; wayward communities, who have become fascinated by the surrounding culture of success, are called back to their own dignity as the people of God; disciples

who have abandoned Jesus are welcomed anew to the community through the gift of his peace. We meet human beings not symbols, people not ciphers, complex individuals not cardboard cut-outs. We come face to face with our ancestors in the faith when they are troubled and exultant; we are drawn into the struggle of their lives; we are moved by their mourning and loss as we are exalted by their daring and faith. It is our own story writ large, which is why it has been proclaimed and read for centuries.

8 The Church has always given a special place to the Bible, particularly in its worship, reflection and preaching: "All the preaching of the Church, as indeed the entire Christian religion, should be nourished and ruled by sacred Scripture."[2] If the real meaning of tradition is not to hold on to something but *to hand on to someone*, the Church has nourished the faithful by handing on the Bible to new generations. The Bible is the foundational document of the Church, and it is a particular mark of the modern Church that it has consistently encouraged the faithful to use the Bible as source for their prayer, ground for their faith, and guide for their everyday living.

---

2. Vatican II, Dogmatic Constitution on Divine Revelation, n.21.

1 FIRST IMAGES OF JESUS

1) The four Gospels are our principal resource for understanding Jesus; they are the foundation documents of our Christian community. Few of us, however, were first introduced to Jesus through reading the Gospels. Most of us were introduced to Jesus through people who passed on to us the living tradition they had received: in that sense the first Gospel we encountered was probably people. The theologian Walter Kasper insists that the starting-point of anyone's faith journey is "faith as it is actually believed, lived, proclaimed and practised in the Christian churches. Faith in Jesus can arise only from encounter with other Christians" (*Jesus the Christ*, p.28). People pass on the faith, they retell the Jesus story "so that you may believe Jesus is the Christ, the Son of God, and believing this, you may have life in his name" (Jn 20:31). As the fourth evangelist reflects, the purpose of passing on the tradition is to give life. Who first introduced us to Jesus? What were our first images of Jesus? Where did those images originate?

Head of Christ:
Leuven, twelfth century

2) **Looking at our own first images of Jesus**

First images of Jesus	Source?
?	parents
?	grandparents
?	parish church
?	school
Yeshua	evangelists

3) Looking at the above panel, you can fill in images of Jesus that were passed on to you from family or institutions. It takes most people time before they meet the Jesus of the evangelists, the one known as Yeshua to his contemporaries. Most people first inherit the images of Jesus that are popular in their family, local tradition, culture, etc. The writers of the Gospels were part of this people-centred process, and they too share their first images of Jesus. If none of the evangelists knew Jesus personally, all of them were introduced to Jesus through an earlier generation of preachers and teachers. Each of them emerged from a different community of faith; each of them passed on, in his own creative way, the living tradition he had received. The Church gave birth to the Gospels, not vice versa.

4) **Looking at the evangelists' first images of Jesus**

At the beginning of each written Gospel, the evangelist connects the new Jesus story to a larger story. Each places the Jesus story into a larger frame: the prophetic story (Mark); the Jewish story (Matthew); the human story (Luke); the divine story (John).

Also, the four evangelists have different first images of Jesus: this is understandable because they begin the story of Jesus in different places. Mark begins with an adult Jesus; Matthew and Luke begin with the conception and birth of Jesus; John begins before the world was created. These different beginnings mean different first images.

First images	Evangelist
Adult layman; Secret Messiah; Suffering Son of Man	Mark
New Moses; Son of David; Son of God	Matthew
Son of David; Son of God	Luke
Logos; Creator of all; Stranger from heaven	John

Mark (c. AD 70): the prophetic story

Context: *back to eighth century*
Mark opens his Gospel by building a bridge back to the Jewish scriptures through the prophecy of Isaiah, from the eighth century BC. That prophecy is secured in the present in the person and ministry of John the Baptist. Jesus first appears on Mark's stage as an adult who leaves home in Nazareth and journeys south to join the multitudes being baptised by the wilderness prophet. The breathless pace of Mark's Gospel begins in the midst of ongoing drama – as ancient prophecy is fulfilled, as John heralds an unknown follower, and as Jesus appears from obscurity to begin his prophetic mission.

Mark, probably the first person to commit the Gospel to writing, tells us nothing of Jesus' previous family life, never even mentioning Joseph. Mark begins Jesus' story at a defining moment in his life, when Jesus leaves home and goes south to the wilderness of Judea. Jesus is an adult layman who leaves Nazareth because he is attracted by the revivalist preaching of John.

For Mark, that initial connection with John the Baptist will define the development of the Jesus story; that contact will make a key difference. As Robert Frost wrote in his poem "The Road not Taken":

I shall be telling you this with a sigh
Somewhere ages and ages hence:
Two roads diverged in a wood,
and I – I took the one less travelled by,
And that has made all the difference.

Piero della Francesca:
Baptism of Christ (detail)

Jesus submits to John's baptism and follows John in the lifestyle of an itinerant prophet. Mark uses the baptism scene to announce to his listeners/readers that Jesus is Son of God. We the readers hear this, but the participants in the story, apart from Jesus, do not. No one in the Gospel will ever refer to this event; no one will ever use the baptism scene as a clue to the identity of Jesus. Later, Mark will develop the story of Jesus' identity through the Suffering Son of Man, used 14 times by Mark and always on Jesus' own lips.

Matthew (c. AD 80): the Jewish story

Context: back to Abraham, nineteenth century BC
Matthew begins his Gospel by announcing the identity of Jesus as "son of David, son of Abraham". He proceeds at a leisurely pace with Abraham, from the nineteenth century BC, and anchors the identity of Jesus in the Jewish tradition as he catalogues the names of Jesus' ancestors. The genealogy is divided into three sections of 14 generations: *the patriarchs*, from Abraham to David; *the kings*, from David to the Babylonian exile; *the unknown people*, from the Babylonian exile to Joseph. Five women are mentioned:

- **Tamar** *(Gen 38)*
- **Rahab** *(Josh 2)*
- **Ruth** *(The Book of Ruth)*
- **Uriah's wife** *(2 Sam 11)*
- **Mary** *(Mt 1:18)*

Looking at the list of names is like leafing through a photograph album of someone's weird and wonderful relatives. God's curious choices include cheats, prostitutes, thieves, adulterers, and murderers – illustrating through biography that God's salvation comes through the foolish and the fragile, the crooked and the cracked. Anyone can play a part in God's plan, which finds its fulfilment in Jesus, who is called Christ.

The first chapter is devoted to names, establishing the *identity* of Jesus. It answers the question: Who is he? The chapter concludes with a double naming: with a quotation from the Hebrew scriptures, establishing his name as Emmanuel, God is with us, and finally with Joseph naming the child Jesus. If the first chapter establishes the identity of Jesus (*Who is he?*) the second chapter establishes the geography (*Where is he from?*). The four quotations from the Hebrew scriptures in the second chapter all focus on geography, placing Jesus originally from *Bethlehem* in Judea, but emerging out of *Egypt*, and eventually settling in *Nazareth*: "He will be called a Nazarene" (2:23). Thus Matthew locates Jesus at the heart of Jewish tradition.

Joseph, like the patriarch Joseph of the Jewish scriptures, is famous as a dreamer and as the one who escapes to Egypt, saving his family. It was Moses who escaped a wicked pharaoh intent on killing all the Hebrew male children.

Gillian Lawson:
The Flight in Egypt

Likewise, in Matthew, Jesus will escape a wicked king intent on murdering all the male children. When Moses is leading his people he is confronted by another wicked king (Num 22-24) who calls a wise man from the east. Three men come, and Balaam, the magus, obeys God rather than the king – as Matthew's magi will later do. Like Moses, Matthew's *new Moses* will come out of Egypt to save his people; like Moses, he will give them the new law from the mountain.

Luke (c. AD 85): the human story
Context: back to Adam, son of God
In his two books, the Gospel and Acts, Luke dramatises history and geography by covering three stages of salvation history:

1) Israel: a narrative recounted in the Law and the Prophets

2) Jesus: a story recounted in the Gospel beginning at 3:1

3) The Church: the story recounted in Acts, beginning at 2:1

Central to Luke's vision is the story of Jesus of Nazareth, binding together the story of Israel and the story of the Church. At the beginning of the Gospel and Acts, Luke builds two bridges. In the first two chapters of the Gospel, four Old Testament characters, Zechariah, Elizabeth, Simeon, and Anna, travel across the bridge to meet the Gospel characters, Mary and Jesus. While their story is focused in sacred space, in the Temple, the story of Jesus transpires in secular space, first in the village of Nazareth and then in the town of Bethlehem. With the infancy stories of John the Baptist and Jesus, Luke attaches the new Israel to the story of old Israel: these two stories meet in the visitation of Mary to Elizabeth.

Later, in his genealogy, Luke presses the ancestry of Jesus back beyond the reaches of the Jewish story to the beginning of the human story in Adam, son of God. This original human connection is grounded in the belief that Jesus is not only the glory of Israel but also a light for all nations. Jesus is not only rooted in the human story, but he comes as a light for the whole of humanity.

The new story is celebrated when Luke introduces the parents of Jesus: Mary is betrothed to Joseph of the **House of David**. This reference goes back to 2 Samuel 7, where David is refused permission to build God a house, but God promises to build David a house.

Leonardo da Vinci:
The Virgin and Child with St Elizabeth and St John the Baptist

2 Samuel 7	Luke 1
9 "I shall make for you a great name…	32a "He will be great… be called Son of the Most High.
13 I shall establish the throne of his kingdom forever	32b And God will give him the throne of his father David;
14 I shall be his father, and he will be my son…	33a and he will be king over the house of Jacob forever.
16 And your house and your kingdom will be secure forever…"	34a and there will be no end to his kingdom."

Where the Bible generally identifies Jerusalem as "the city of David" Luke is unique in identifying David's city as Bethlehem. The annunciation to the shepherds declares: "To you this day there is born in the city of David a messiah who is Christ the Lord." David was a shepherd in Bethlehem before he became the saviour of his people; the first visitors to the *Son of David*, unsurprisingly, are shepherds, not magi. The original son of David was Solomon, who declared that when he was born, he was nurtured in swaddling clothes: "No *king* has known any other beginning of existence" (Wis 7:5). The new *Son of David* will have the same beginning.

Thus Luke proclaims in his infancy narrative that Jesus is **Son of David** and **Son of God**. The proclamation of Jesus' identity as Son of God is one that Luke now applies to the *birth* of Jesus, where the earlier preaching of Paul applied it to his *resurrection* (see Rom 1:3-4).

Sculpture: *Water of Life, by Stephen Broadbent. Jesus and the Woman of Samaria, set in the Cloister Garden of Chester Cathedral*

John (c. AD 100): the divine story

Context: before the beginning of the world

John's Gospel begins not with an adult Jesus by the River Jordan or a newborn baby in Bethlehem, but before the beginning of the world. For John, the details of Jesus' earthly beginnings are irrelevant – no birth is mentioned, no mother is introduced, no time is recorded, no place is noted, no witnesses are named – because his true origin is beyond the cosmos: "In the beginning was the Word, and the Word was with God, and the Word was God."

John goes back beyond the prophetic story and the Jewish story and the human story, to rework Genesis and anchor the beginning of the Jesus story in the originality of God. You can see the echoes of Genesis in John's Prologue: in the beginning, God, the word, life, light, and darkness.

Genesis 1: In the beginning God created the heavens and the earth. Now the earth was a formless void, there was darkness over the deep, and God's spirit hovered over the waters. God said: "Let there be light", and there was light. God saw that the light was good, and separated the light from the darkness.

John 1: In the beginning was the Word, the Word was with God and the Word was God. He was with God in the beginning. Through him all things came to be, not one thing had its being but through him. All that came to be had life in him and that life is the light of all people, a light that shines in the dark, a light that darkness could not overpower.

John establishes the true context of Jesus as one that is beyond this world, in the divine realm of light. He is the wisdom from above and descends into human history. The historical setting for the Gospel is, of course, in this world of time and place. This double context for the story of Jesus will be played out ironically when Jesus meets the woman of Samaria and throughout the whole movement of this Gospel.

After establishing the divine origins of Jesus in the Prologue, the evangelist then introduces John as a witness to the light, identifying him by the negative assertion: "He was not the light." He then returns to the Word as the true light that enlightens all peoples. For the fourth evangelist, the story of Jesus is part of a larger story that began with creation and has been continuing ever since the beginning.

The pre-existent Word experiences rejection from the world he created and from his own people who do not receive him, but he empowers all those who accept him as God's children. The narrator finally becomes personal in celebrating that the Word became flesh "among us". The prologue that began outside human experience, *before the beginning of creation*, now moves to the experience of *the Christian community* in its testimony: "we saw his glory", a testimony that is confirmed by the witness of John the Baptist.

The word has universal authority, acknowledged and asserted from the beginning. The image is always individual and specific, forced to opt for one aspect only out of the many that we know exist... Images are inadequate, but the answer is not to ban them but to multiply to infinity the opportunities for contemplation that they afford.

Neil MacGregor, Director of the National Gallery
The Image of Christ: Catalogue of the Exhibition, Seeing Salvation (London, 2000) p. 7

FURTHER READING

D. McBride,   "Where does the Jesus story begin?"
The Tablet, Christmas edition, 2000

P. Fredriksen,   *From Jesus to Christ* (London: Yale University Press, 2000) pp.18-61

M. Hooker,   *Beginnings: Keys that Open the Gospels* (London: SCM, 1997)

D. Allison,   *The New Moses: a Matthean Typology* (Edinburgh: T & T Clark, 1993)

F. Moloney,   *Beginning the Good News: a Narrative Approach* (Homebush: St Paul's, 1992)

UNCOVERING THE ORIGINAL RELATIONSHIP

2

1) At the beginning of Christianity there stands a relationship, not just a person. Some people came into contact with Jesus of Nazareth, something happened to them, and they were changed. They experienced new life, they felt understood, they felt challenged. Others, however, reacted with aggressive disapproval, which culminated in the death of Jesus. What Jesus came to mean for the early Christian community is reflected in the pages of the Gospel. Jesus does not come to us alone; he comes to us via the reflective faith of the Christian community.

2) None of the evangelists writes an essay about the public ministry of Jesus; they all recount narratives of the Jesus story, developing their accounts through what Jesus does and says and how other people react to what he offers. All four evangelists write stories of people's positive encounter with Jesus: *(see figure 1)*

People's new experience is turned into a story; it is interpreted as a message of salvation. People's experience of Jesus is not just a personal story of change; it leads them to make *claims* about Jesus "Given what happened to me, who then is he?" As the evangelists teach us, we learn about Jesus through those who have life in his name.

3) The people who have new life in Jesus' name become our teachers. In traditional religious worlds the teachers are usually male clerics; in the Gospel world the teachers are those who have been touched by Jesus. There is a shift from the experience of authority (chief priests and scribes) to the authority of experience (those who have been touched by Jesus). Their authority is not from learning but from their own experience: "I only know I was blind and now I can see" (Jn 9:25). The people recommended by the Gospel as our teachers make up an unusual list. For example:

- The woman of Samaria
- The demoniac
- A child
- The woman who anoints Jesus at dinner

figure 1.

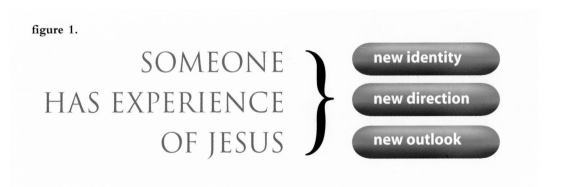

SOMEONE HAS EXPERIENCE OF JESUS } new identity / new direction / new outlook

However unlikely they might first appear as evangelists, these are the kind of people the Gospel presents to us as teachers about Jesus.

4) **The call of discipleship: comparing three traditions**

All four Gospels tell us not only the story of Jesus but also the story of discipleship; they paint a picture of the fortunes and failings of Jesus' own followers as they struggle to remain attached to the person of Jesus and devoted to his mission. Throughout the Gospels the story of discipleship is closely intertwined with the story of Jesus, and no evangelist offers the story of Jesus without the story of his community. How does discipleship begin? What moves people to leave the security of what they are doing, to risk themselves in a new venture where they believe they are being "called" to do something for God? How does this call manifest itself?

The fourth-century white synagogue in Capernaum. Beneath the remains are the black basalt stones that formed the foundation for the synagogue of Jesus.

Mark's account (1:16–20)

In Mark the call of the disciples is brief, bold and unelaborated. The arrest of John the Baptist prompts Jesus to begin preaching in Galilee, where without introduction or notice he calls the first disciples. It is a command rather than an invitation, and it is presented as an exclusive act of Jesus' own initiative. As E. Best comments: "Jesus appears suddenly out of the blue and calls Peter and Andrew to be his disciples. There has been no psychological or other preparation" (*Mark: The Gospel as Story* (Edinburgh: T & T Clark, 1983) p.83).

The first four disciples are identified as fishermen, and they are seen actively engaged in their normal round of work when a stranger's imperative interrupts them. The call of Jesus offers them not only a new identity as "fishers of men" – a somewhat peculiar image, given what fishermen do to fish when they catch them – but also a new direction in life, one that will be determined by Jesus himself.

Mark's account displays no interest in emotional or biographical details; rather, having begun his Gospel with an adult Jesus, he is clearly anxious to advance the narrative by illustrating Jesus' ability to command ready and absolute allegiance. No personal motive is ascribed to the disciples for becoming followers; no speech is attributed to them by way of a response; rather, their answer is illustrated by what they do in leaving their nets (Peter and Andrew) and their own people (James and John) to follow the command of Jesus.

Luke's account (5:1-11)

Where Mark's account of the call of the first disciples is abrupt and staccato, Luke's is expansive and connective. Luke bides his time, first showing Jesus ministering alone in Galilee. The rejection of Jesus by his own townspeople accounts for Jesus' compulsive move elsewhere, and Luke will transpose Mark's implausible account of the call of the first disciples to an event following Jesus' ministry in the lakeside town of Capernaum. Here he ministers to the local people, preaches in their synagogue, and cures many sick people, including Simon's mother-in-law (Lk 4:31-41). When the townspeople try to prevent Jesus from leaving, he explains he must go to preach in other towns. Alone he leaves Capernaum for Judea (4:44); he has yet to call anyone to be his disciple.

Luke builds up a relationship between Jesus and the local townspeople who, unlike the people of Nazareth, are unfamiliar with his family and background: it is as if Luke illustrates the adage that an expert is someone from a different village. When Jesus returns to the shores of the lakeside, he preaches from Simon's boat. Again Luke connects the two men as friends. Over against Mark's far-fetched account of Jesus calling strangers, Luke has provided a setting where the first disciples, before being called, witness for themselves the power of Jesus' deeds and words in their town, thus providing a psychologically credible setting for the call. This is further established by Luke's use of the miraculous catch of fish as part of his pronouncement story of the call of Simon, which leads to the climactic commission: "Do not be afraid; from now on you will be catching people" (Lk 5:11).

John's account (1:35-42)

John's account goes in a wholly different direction (Jn 1:35-51). Jesus attaches himself to the Baptist movement on the far side of the Jordan and is later identified to John: "Rabbi, the one who was with you across the Jordan, to whom you testified, here he is baptising, and all are going to him" (Jn 3:26). As J. Murphy-O'Connor comments: "How long Jesus spent with John should not be underestimated. At least sufficient time has to be allowed for some of the Baptist's disciples to transfer their allegiance to Jesus. According to the Fourth Gospel, this process took only three days (1:29-51), but the schematic character of the presentation is obvious" ("John the Baptist and Jesus: History and Hypotheses" in *New Testament Studies* 36 (1990), p.362).

Jesus' first disciples clearly come from the Baptist movement. When John identifies Jesus as the lamb of God, two disciples decide to follow Jesus on their own initiative. "When Jesus turned and saw them following him, he said to them, 'What are you looking for?' They said to him, 'Rabbi, where are you staying?' He said to them, 'Come and see.' They came and saw where he was staying, and they remained with him that day" (Jn 1:38-39). Andrew is identified as one of these two disciples, and he brings his brother Simon into the presence of Jesus.

Luke provides us with a story to explain the **impact** Jesus had on the first disciples.
The Gospels are punctuated with stories that show the impact Jesus made on people.
This impact, by necessity, *preceded* people's interest in Jesus.

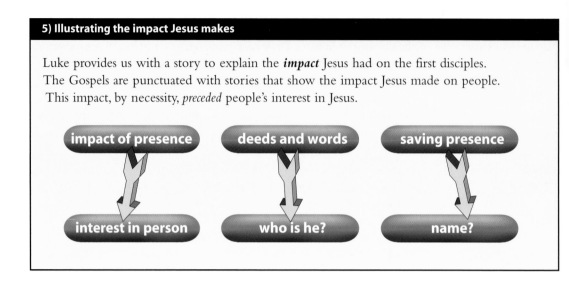

6) Because of what Jesus does, because of the things that happen through him, because of what he sets in motion, because of what he says, *then* there is the question, *"Who is this man who...?"* Because of Jesus' actions (verbs), people wonder who he (the subject of the verb) is. If Jesus had done and said the same as all the other rabbis and leaders, no one would have been moved to ask the question about why *he* was different. **People move from experiencing his saving presence to wondering about his real identity.** Given what he does, who is he? It is a reflection of the impact Jesus makes on people that they become interested in his name, his identity. *(Contrast this with classical Christology and its disinterest in the historical Jesus.)*

7) In presenting Jesus to their readers, the evangelists catalogue a variety of reactions to him. We hear *different* voices speak about Jesus:

- some speak words of wonder and gratitude
- others register their confusion
- a large group speak in the language of opposition and threat

People name Jesus according to their experience of him: some are delighted in him; some are challenged by him; some feel threatened by him. Throughout the Gospel narratives people's response to Jesus is determined by how they interpret their experience of him. From their experience they decide on a name to give him. That "name" will determine how they respond to him.

There are different responses to the question: Who do you say that I am?

He is mad	take charge of him	He is anti-clerical	watch him
He is our healer	keep him	He is Son of David	appeal to him
He is our master	learn from him	He is a glutton and a drunk	avoid him
He is a teacher	listen to him	He is a blasphemer	condemn him
He is the devil's agent	oppose him	He is wanted by the police	betray him
He is a friend of sinners	denounce him	He is finished	leave him
He is a prophet	heed him	He is dangerous to know	deny him
He is the Messiah	follow him	He is a criminal	execute him
He feeds us	crown him	He is a fake	mock him
He is forgiving	talk to him	He is suffering	weep for him
He is crazy	ignore him	He is innocent	support him
He is a man of God	respect him	He is risen	worship him

FURTHER READING

N.T. Wright and M. Borg,	*The Meaning of Jesus* (London: SPCK, 2000) pp.3-27
B. Chilton,	"Friends and Enemies" in *The Cambridge Companion to Jesus* (Cambridge: Cambridge University Press, 2001) chapter 5

Participants following the course on Jesus and Discipleship at Hawkstone Hall

Top Left:
Karl & Josephine Desouza, from Singapore

Left:
Fr Gerard Byaruhanga, from Uganda

Right:
A section of the international group

FASCINATION & DISCIPLESHIP: A REFLECTION

All four Gospels tell us not only the story of Jesus but also the story of discipleship; they paint a picture of the fortunes and failings of Jesus' own community. Throughout the Gospels the story of discipleship is told alongside the story of Jesus. How does discipleship begin? What moves people to leave whatever they are doing, to risk themselves in a new venture where they believe they are being "called" to do something for God. How does this call manifest itself?

Dissatisfaction

Sometimes people experience a lingering dissatisfaction with what they are doing, the way their life is moving. They feel that what they are doing, however worthwhile, is some-how not enough. Rather than passively accept this dissatisfaction as part of life, as something that has to be endured, some people see it as a signal to move on. They interpret their experience as a sign that they should look elsewhere, try something different, be open to new possibilities. When this happens their dissatisfaction becomes a positive experience; it leads them to look beyond the boundaries of their own life, to dream of other roads that could be taken. Of course being attracted to another way of life usually makes for dissatisfaction with the present situation.

Fascination

The story of faith often begins with fascination: we are attracted by what we see about another person, at the level of the human. This fascination is different from curiosity about a person: we may be curious about how some people become rich, where sailors sleep in submarines, or how the man who clears the snow drifts drives to work. This is curiosity. The fascination of faith is related to how people actually live; it becomes fired by interest in the way another person relates and how that individual looks at life. The fascination of faith is drawn by another person's way of being human, the other person's way of being alive.

In the Gospels we see Jesus minister to a variety of people: many people acknowledge that what Jesus does and says, his deeds and words, are different from the usual things they witness around them. What *he* does stands out; what *he* says is liberating: "He teaches with authority, not like the scribes" (Mk 1:22). Some people are astonished by Jesus' ministry, but they have no desire to be engaged by it; they do not feel claimed by what they experience.

What they witness is out there to be admired and applauded, but it does not call out to them, it does not have their name written on it. Their astonishment may lead to praise, and then they go home. They go away praising God, and the story stops there.

What they saw and heard was fascinating, but it makes no further claim on their attention or on their lives. This is not unlike seeing a play or a film that is inspiring and enjoyable at the time, but then quickly falls into forgetfulness. A month later we can hardly remember the characters or the plot. Someone or something can momentarily fascinate us, but the experience can fail to leave any lasting impression: life continues as usual.

Desire

Some people are attracted to what fascinates them, and when this occurs their fascination moves to desire. Sometimes fascination forces us to pause, to stop what we are doing: we reflect; we want to pursue this experience; we want to claim it in our own lives. When we feel that desire we become apprentices and try to attach ourselves to the person who inspired us. We want to make the original experience a part of our lives. What we have seen and heard is no longer something to admire from a distance, it is now something to participate in, a new life that we want a share in ourselves. We do not walk away or go home; we *follow* what we find fascinating.

The difference between fascination and desire is explored in the Parable of the Sower, where the rocky soil represents fascination by itself and the good soil represents desire. The seed the farmer throws on the rocky ground is welcomed readily with joy. People are fascinated by it and they say yes, but they have no ground to receive the seed and make it their own. The good soil represents those people who listen to the word and take it to heart: their fascination moves to desire in wanting to make the gift their own. Thus the soil and the seed join together and make something new (Mk 4:14-20).

- *Can you think of any Gospel stories where an individual's fascination with Jesus moves to desire and attachment?*

- *Can you think of someone in your own life who made a deep impression on you and who also made a significant difference to the direction of your life?*

Distance

The fascination that we originally experience can change: we now want distance rather than closeness; we now want to create space and separation between ourselves and the one who first fascinated us. Luke illustrates this in his call story of Simon (Lk 5:3-11). With Jesus' move to Capernaum, he has become well known and accepted by the people of the fishing village. He preaches in their synagogue and makes Simon's house his headquarters as he makes Simon's boat his pulpit. But when Simon personally experiences the power of the Lord in his own life his attraction to Jesus moves in the opposite direction: "Leave me alone, Lord; I am a sinful man."

Envy

Fascination and astonishment can move to envy. We want to destroy what fascinates us; we are drawn by the experience but because of a deep sense of our own worthlessness we reject the invitation. A good example of this appears in Luke's narrative about Jesus' return to Nazareth (Lk 4:16-30). When Jesus finishes preaching in the synagogue the first reaction of his hearers is astonishment and admiration. But the audience moves quickly from astonishment at Jesus' preaching to focusing on their familiarity with him, the neighbour, the local man, whose family they all know. They wonder where Jesus picked up all the wisdom that he is now sharing. What has been granted to *him* that has been denied them? Why is *he* so different?

The reaction of Jesus' neighbours is fairly typical of agrarian village life. In most traditional villages, where everyone knows everyone else, the secret of survival is to be like everyone else. If anyone emerges as different, if anyone raises his or her head above the others, that individual is likely to lose it. Difference disturbs the equilibrium, the sameness of village life.

Like Joseph in the Old Testament who wore technicolour clothes and saw things in dreams others did not see: his brothers' envy led them to dismiss him and exile him to Egypt.

Jesus suffers the same fate of exile. Jesus left the village an ordinary workman; when he returns from his time with John the Baptist he projects a new identity, that of the wandering prophet. The people can accept Jesus the workman, but they cannot accept Jesus the prophet. Their original admiration turns to envy, and their envy moves to violence: wanting to destroy Jesus' difference, they take him to the top of a hill and try to throw him. Later the envy of the chief priests will also shift to violence when they hand Jesus over to the civil authorities for execution (see Mk 15:10).

The origin of power

Sometimes we meet people who touch us by their vision, their way of being human, people who intrigue us by their power. Jesus never claims to be the origin of the power that shows itself in his ministry. He tells people to give praise to God for what they have experienced or witnessed: "Go home to your people and tell them all that God in his mercy has done for you" (Mk 5:19).

In his dealings with other people, in the surface events of every day, Jesus opens up another dimension, that people cannot see, namely his relationship to God whom he calls Abba. Both dimensions of Jesus' life – the horizontal and the vertical – are open to others.

Many people, especially Jesus' religious critics, want to know by what authority Jesus does what he does and says what he says. Who is the *author* of this power? Jesus claims that God was the source of his liberating power: "If it is by the finger of God that I cast out devils, then the kingdom of God has overtaken you" (Lk 11:20).

Jesus leads his disciples to the source of his power and strength. Not surprisingly, his disciples want to be in touch with that same source, which is why they ask Jesus to teach them to pray. Jesus teaches them to connect to his Abba, who is also theirs: "When you pray say this: 'Abba…'"

Discipleship or slavery

Early in the Gospel of John the disciples ask Jesus: "Where do you live?" And his reply is, "Come and see." The place where Jesus lives is no secret; it is a home to be shared with others. Going to see is the initial movement from fascination and desire into discipleship. This is the movement that goes beyond being fascinated with the person to trying to understand and participate in the person's life and power. It is to experience and to share the place where the master really lives.

The essence of discipleship is an introduction to the power the master has, so that the disciples can live in the same power. The eyes of the apprentice must be opened, the ears unstopped, the heart educated to the power that makes the master the master.

Jesus opens up another dimension, that people cannot see, namely his relationship to God whom he calls Abba. Both dimensions of Jesus' life (the horizontal and the vertical) are open to others.

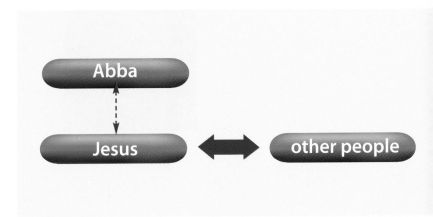

The purpose of the master is not to mystify the power, but to open it up to apprentices. Some masters keep their power a secret, thus keeping others in perpetual dependence. When this happens, disciples end up feeling like slaves, caught in perpetual admiration for a power they cannot share and an authority they can never exercise.

In contrast Jesus fosters the greatness of his own disciples; he wants them to become masters in their own turn, so that they will do greater things than he has managed to do:

> *"Whoever believes in me will perform the same works as myself, he will perform even greater works." (Jn 14:12)*

> *"I call you friends, since I have made known to you everything I have learned from my Father." (Jn 15:15)*

Jesus thus becomes a mentor to his own disciples, preparing them for the day when they will be masters who will continue to pass on his message and move in the same power that animated him. This is the lively meaning of *tradition*, the act of handing over to others what one has received oneself.

Thus the Christian story continues to be told and lived by power-sharers not power-keepers, by people like Jesus who hope that new generations will do greater things than they have done.

FOLLOWER BY SEAMUS HEANEY

My father worked with a horse-plough,
His shoulders globed like a full sail strung
Between the shafts and the furrow.
The horses strained at his clicking tongue.

An expert. He would set the wing
And fit the bright steel-pointed sock.
The sod rolled over without breaking.
At the headrig, with a single pluck

Of reins, the sweating team turned round
And back into the land. His eye
Narrowed and angled at the ground,
Mapping the furrow exactly.

I stumbled in his hob-nailed wake,
Fell sometimes on the polished sod;
Sometimes he rode me on his back
Dipping and rising to his plod.

I wanted to grow up and plough,
To close one eye, stiffen my arm.
All I ever did was follow
In his broad shadow round the farm.

I was a nuisance, tripping, falling,
Yapping always. But today
It is my father who keeps stumbling
Behind me, and will not go away.

Seamus Heaney, **New Selected Poems**
1966-1987 *(London: Faber & Faber, 1988) p.6*

FURTHER READING

D. McBride,   "Reflections on Discipleship" in *Scripture Bulletin 30*
                     (July 2000) pp.30-38

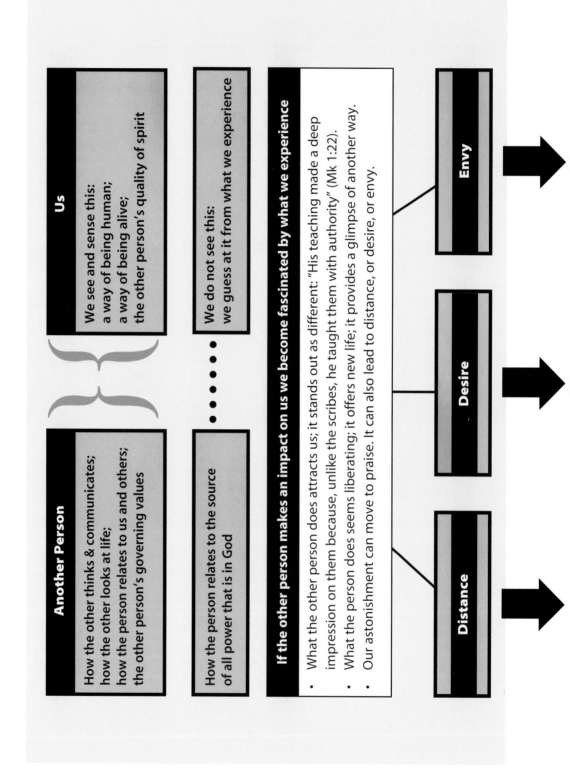

Another Person

How the other thinks & communicates;
how the other looks at life;
how the person relates to us and others;
the other person's governing values

How the person relates to the source
of all power that is in God

Us

We see and sense this:
a way of being human;
a way of being alive;
the other person's quality of spirit

We do not see this:
we guess at it from what we experience

If the other person makes an impact on us we become fascinated by what we experience

- What the other person does attracts us; it stands out as different: "His teaching made a deep impression on them because, unlike the scribes, he taught them with authority" (Mk 1:22).
- What the person does seems liberating; it offers new life; it provides a glimpse of another way.
- Our astonishment can move to praise. It can also lead to distance, or desire, or envy.

Envy

Desire

Distance

We protect ourselves from the transparent goodness of the other; we disconnect

a) When Simon Peter saw this he fell at the knees of Jesus, saying: "Leave me alone, Lord; I am a sinful man." (Lk 5:8)

b) After this many of his disciples left Jesus and stopped going with him. Then Jesus said to the Twelve: "What about you, do you want to go away too?" (Jn 6:66-67)

c) The face of the rich young man fell at these words and he went away sad, for he was a man of great wealth. (Mk 10:22)

We claim the experience as part of our own story; we connect with the other person

a) Leaving their father Zebedee in the boat with the men he employed, James and John went after Jesus. (Mk 1:20)

b) As Jesus was getting into the boat, the man who had been possessed begged Jesus to stay with him. (Mk 5:18)

c) Your personal story… the account of your own attachment to an authoritative figure in your life or to Jesus of Nazareth.

We discredit what secretly fascinates us; envy can then move to violence

a) Herod said: "Go and find all about the child, and when you have found him, let me know, so that I too may go and do him homage." (Mt 2:8)

b) The people sprang to their feet and hustled Jesus out of the town; and they took him to the brow of the hill, intending to throw him down the cliff. (Lk 4:29)

c) For Pilate realised that it was out of jealousy that the chief priests had handed Jesus over. (Mk 15:10)

out of desire

Discipleship

Teacher passes on authority.
Authority *authors* new life and shares power.
Disciples are gradually empowered to become teachers.

"Whoever believes in me will perform the same works as myself, he will perform even greater works." (Jn 14:12)

"I no longer speak to you as slaves, for a slave does not know his master's business. Instead, I call you friends, since I have made known to you all that I learned from my Father." (Jn 15:15)

Slavery

Teacher retains power.
Authority figure does not share the source of power but keeps others dependent.
People feel gradually diminished.

"You may think of yourself as good; indeed the time might come when you may even approach greatness. But believe me when I tell you that you will never be as great as I am."

4 BEGINNING WITH THE PASSION & DEATH

"Why start the quest of the historical Jesus with his death? Because, quite simply, the death of Jesus is central in every way... the one great incident in the life of Jesus on this lean earth which interests Paul, the first great propagandist for the Jesus movement whose writings we possess, is the death of Jesus. Round the dual focus of the death and resurrection of Jesus, all Paul's teaching and preaching evolves. And this is surely because the death of Jesus is in fact central to every form of expression and practice of the religion he founded.

For it is almost as true of the other synoptic Gospels as D.E. Nineham once said of Mark, that they are like tadpoles, with large heads composed of the so-called Passion narratives, weaving behind them longer but much thinner tales. So is the death of Jesus the central focus of the New Testament as a whole. Likewise, it is quite literally at the centre of those other great and authoritative expressions of the essence of Christianity, the oldest and most popular of the creeds."

(J.P. Mackey, *Jesus, the Man and the Myth*, pp. 51-54)

1) The death and resurrection form the central Christian proclamation about Jesus, a truth that is celebrated in the principal eucharistic prayers:

i. Father, we celebrate the memory of Christ, your Son. We, your people and your ministers, recall his *passion, his resurrection from the dead...*

ii. In memory of *his death and resurrection,* we offer you, Father, this life-giving bread...

iii. Father, calling to mind *the death* your Son endured for our salvation...

iv. We recall Christ's *death*, his descent among the dead, *his resurrection...*

2) The centrality of the death and resurrection is reflected in the preaching of the early Church. While Jesus focused on the kingdom of God, the apostolic preachers focus on Jesus himself. In the words of Bultmann, "the preacher becomes the preached". You can see a gradual change in the preached Gospel from Jesus to the last evangelist. As the tradition develops the story of Jesus is enlarged, but the focus on the last days of Jesus remains the same:

Gospel	Focus
Jesus	kingdom of God
apostolic preachers	*death & resurrection of Jesus*
Mark	ministry; *death & resurrection*
Matthew & Luke	infancy; ministry; *death & resurrection*
John	prologue; ministry; *death & resurrection*

The centrality of the death of Jesus is reflected in our principal Christian image of Jesus, a dying man on a cross. This enduring image carries its own teaching: whoever you believe Jesus to be, depends on how you interpret his death.

It may seem strange to begin looking at the story of Jesus with his passion, death and resurrection, but this reflects where the early Church began its preaching about Jesus. In a sense none of us is complete until our death; the whole story cannot be told about us until we have finished it. The same is true of Jesus. More importantly, the death of Jesus is central to the understanding of who he is. For the four evangelists, the passion is the target towards which the entire Gospel moves.

3) In the earliest Gospel, when people ask Jesus *who he is*, he tells them *where he must go.* When people ask about his *identity*, he tells them about his *destiny*: that he must suffer and be rejected by the chief priests and the elders, and be put to death. In Mark, the disciples do not come to understand Jesus in his lifetime. Nobody understands Jesus until after his death. And only then does a human being, for the first time, announce who he is. This person is not a disciple, but a pagan soldier: "Truly this man was Son of God."

The identity of Jesus is known only when his destiny is fulfilled on the cross

Craigie Aitchison:
Crucifixion 1984

New Experience or Story

PROPHECY
(old story)

New Interpretation

4) In each Gospel, the longest story about Jesus is the story of his passion and death. It is the one part of the Gospels where there is most agreement. Scholars will argue that these are the *oldest* part of the Gospels, the oldest stories about Jesus. Narratives about Jesus' death were formed very quickly in the Christian communities: the setting that formed them was probably liturgical recitation of the final hours of Jesus, and many of the Old Testament readings and prayers would have been integrated into the story. This puts the event of Jesus' death into the larger context of prophecy.

The message is clear: what has happened was not an accident; it was meant to be.

5) The details of the passion story have been bonded so closely with allusions to the Old Testament that it is sometimes difficult to tell where the story finishes and the allusions begin. In the crucifixion scene alone, we find Old Testament allusions for the following details of Mark's account:

- *the offer of wine (Ps 69);*
- *the division of Jesus' garments (Ps 22);*
- *the presence of two robbers (Is 63);*
- *the reactions of the mockers (Ps 22; Wis 2);*
- *the darkness (Amos 8);*
- *Jesus' final prayer (Ps 22);*
- *the offer of vinegar (Ps 69);*
- *the loud cry of Jesus (Ps 31);*
- *the tearing of the Temple veil (Ex 26).*

The evangelists are not just reporting history, but presenting their interpretation in the perspective of faith and prophecy. They search the scriptures to help them make sense of new events.

6) Most of the Gospel stories have no fixed time and place: they are oral traditions about Jesus that the evangelists have collected and reshaped into their major narrative. These passages are often referred to as *pericopes* – coming from the Greek word *peri/koptein*: around/to cut.

7) The passion narratives, however, follow an in-built chronological sequence:

- the arrest
- the interrogation by the high priest
- the trials before the Sanhedrin and Pontius Pilate
- the condemnation
- the crucifixion
- the death
- the burial

That continuity makes for a structured narrative, which is not true of the rest of the Gospel, composed of collections of deeds and sayings of Jesus in no particular sequence. All four evangelists reflect a continuity in agreement in the passion accounts unparalleled elsewhere in the Gospels. Each evangelist, however, exercises his own editorial control over his sources, giving his own perspective and interpretation of the passion and death of Jesus. The evangelists are not focused on writing what we would regard as a modern historical account; they are preaching a message about the meaning of Jesus' death.

8) The passion is written as a story that is larger than Jesus' story. Over half of the narratives concern other people and what happens to them. Their reactions are an integral part of the story: the responses of the disciples, Judas, Peter, the authorities, Caiaphas, the witnesses, Herod Antipas, Pilate, the bystanders, the women, the centurion, the soldiers etc. are noted. In that way the readers are drawn into the narrative, as if faced with the question: "Where would we be in this story? Who would we stand beside?" We will concentrate on the disciples' reactions.

In the Synoptic Gospels the overall pattern of the **Jesus story** in his ministry, passion and death, and resurrection is told alongside the overall pattern of the **disciples' story**. In the ministry of Jesus, the principal relationship between Jesus and the disciples is attachment; that changes in the passion and death to separation and loss; the story of Jesus' resurrection is told through the refounding of the community and their new attachment to Jesus as Lord.

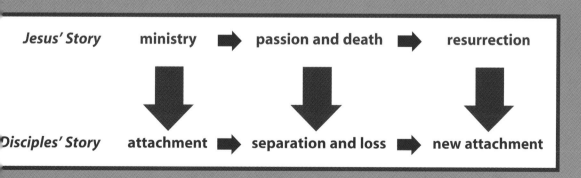

Jesus' Story   ministry ➡ passion and death ➡ resurrection

Disciples' Story   attachment ➡ separation and loss ➡ new attachment

THE PASSION
Jerusalem: brief geographical notes

Mount of Olives

Lying east of the city of Jerusalem, the Mount of Olives is a two-mile ridge, rising some 100 metres above the city. At various points it provides magnificent views over the city. When in Jerusalem, Jesus stayed with his friends in Bethany, and Bethphage was the starting-point of his triumphal entry into Jerusalem. The Roman legions gathered on the Mount of Olives for the siege of Jerusalem in AD 70; their leader, Titus, camped at the highest point, called Mount Scopus, so named because it affords the visitor coming from Jericho the first sight of the city of Jerusalem. The concentration of cemeteries (Christian and Jewish) on the south-western slope of the Mount is because of the belief that the Kidron is the Valley of Jehoshaphat where the whole of humanity will assemble to be judged by God (see Joel 3:2; Zech 14:4).

Valley of the Kidron

The Valley of the Kidron is situated just east of the old walled city of Jerusalem, separating it from the Mount of Olives. The name Kidron seems to mean "dark" or "unclear" - possibly a reference to the sediment stirred up by the winter stream that flowed there. At the time of Jesus, the entire east side of the Kidron Valley was a vast cemetery, and you can still see some of the ancient tombs carved out of the rocks. On the first Holy Thursday, although Jesus and his disciples crossed the valley in late evening, the time of Passover would have meant a full moon, since the feast is a lunar one. This makes the setting for the beginning of the passion a sombre one: Jesus and his disciples walk through the graveyard of the Valley of the Kidron, arguing about how the disciples will conduct themselves during the impending crisis (Mk 14:26-31).

The Garden of Gethsemane

The name Gethsemane derives from the Hebrew and Aramaic words for "oil press" or "oil stores". Neither Luke nor John mentions Gethsemane by name; while Luke speaks of a place (*topos*) on the Mount of Olives, only John identifies it as a garden or enclosure (*kepos*). In all likelihood Gethsemane consisted of an olive grove and a press to crush the olives. According to Josephus, all the olive trees to the east of Jerusalem were cut down and used as tinder for burning the city in AD 70 (Josephus, *War*, 6.1.1). Since an olive grove is not the kind of place that would leave identifiable archaeological remains, the precise place cannot be determined, even if the general area can be securely known. About the year 380 the Byzantine Church of the Agony was built around a rock where it was thought Jesus prayed, which is where the modern Church of All Nations, seen on the right, now stands.

Golgotha

Golgotha, meaning "place of the skull", was outside one of the west gates of Jerusalem; it was not, as the hymn tells us, "a green hill far away". The Fourth Gospel stresses that many Jews read the inscription on the cross "because the place was near the city" (Jn 19:20). The area of Golgotha was included within Jerusalem's city walls by King Herod Agrippa I (AD 40-44). After Jerusalem had been destroyed in AD 135, the new city was rebuilt further to the north, so that the site of Golgotha ended up in the centre of the city. Today it is within the Basilica of the Holy Sepulchre.

The Church of All Nations:
*at the base of the Mount of Olives, with the
Garden of Gethsemane seen on the left*

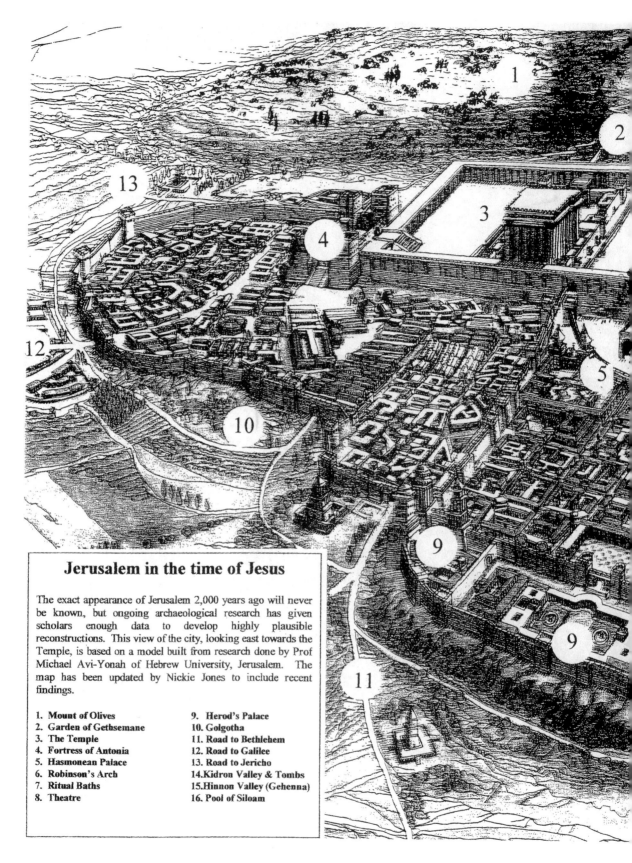

Jerusalem in the time of Jesus

The exact appearance of Jerusalem 2,000 years ago will never be known, but ongoing archaeological research has given scholars enough data to develop highly plausible reconstructions. This view of the city, looking east towards the Temple, is based on a model built from research done by Prof Michael Avi-Yonah of Hebrew University, Jerusalem. The map has been updated by Nickie Jones to include recent findings.

1. **Mount of Olives**
2. **Garden of Gethsemane**
3. **The Temple**
4. **Fortress of Antonia**
5. **Hasmonean Palace**
6. **Robinson's Arch**
7. **Ritual Baths**
8. **Theatre**
9. **Herod's Palace**
10. **Golgotha**
11. **Road to Bethlehem**
12. **Road to Galilee**
13. **Road to Jericho**
14. **Kidron Valley & Tombs**
15. **Hinnon Valley (Gehenna)**
16. **Pool of Siloam**

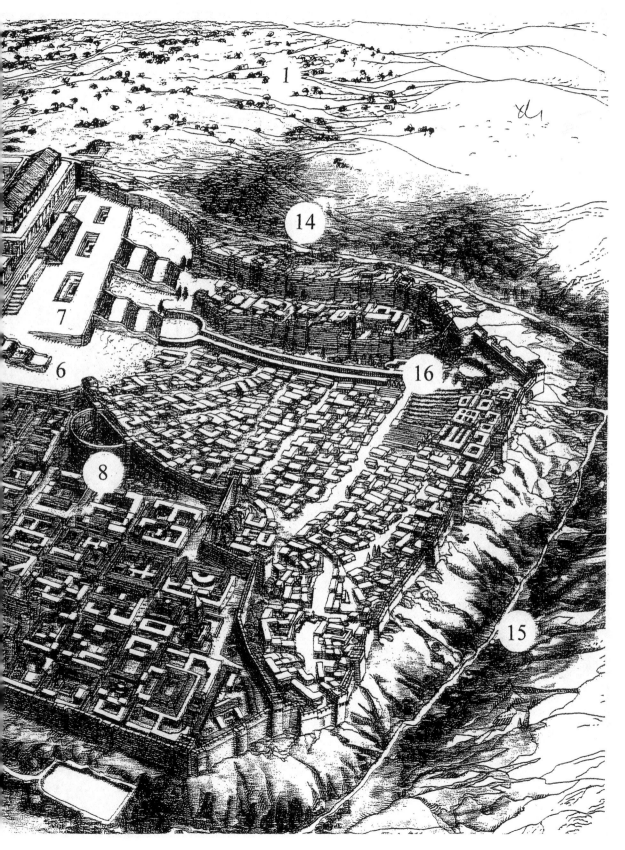

Mark

Jesus' view of disciples

14:27 "You will all lose faith"

- Peter's protest
- Prophecy of Peter's denial
- Peter's earnest protest: "I will never disown you"
- All say the same.

Gethsemane 14:32

- Jesus says to the disciples: "Sit here, while I pray"
- Takes Peter, James, John. He is greatly distressed and troubled: "My soul is very sorrowful… remain and watch"
- Goes farther, falls on ground, and prays the hour might pass

"Abba, Father, all things are possible for you, remove this cup; yet not what I will but what you will"

1. Goes to disciples and finds them asleep. Speaks to Simon. Returns and prays the same words.
2. He comes back and finds the disciples sleeping; they do not know what to answer him.
3. He comes a third time: "Still sleeping? It is enough. Rise up. See, my betrayer is at hand."

Matthew

Jesus' view of disciples

26:30

Parallel to Mark

Gethsemane 26:36

- Parallel to Mark
- Takes Peter and two sons of Zebedee
- Goes farther, falls on face

"My Father, if it be possible let this cup pass from me; Nevertheless, not as I will be as you will"

1. Parallel to Mark
2. Leaves them again. He goes away and prays for a third time, saying the same words.
3. Parallel to Mark

Luke

Jesus' view of disciples

22:28 "You stood by me faithfully in my trials… you will sit on thrones…"

- Prophecy of Peter's denial
- but "once you have recovered you must return and strengthen your brothers"

Usual place on Mt Olives 22:39

- Jesus says to disciples: "Pray not to be put to the test"
- Withdraws from them, kneels and prays

"Father, if you are willing, remove this cup from me; nevertheless not my will, but yours, be done"

Angel appears and strengthens him. Being in *agonia*, he prays more earnestly. His sweat is like great drops of blood. Rises, comes to disciples, finds them sleeping for sorrow. "Why do you sleep? Rise and pray that you may not enter into temptation."

John

Jesus' view of disciples

13:38 Prophecy of Peter's denial

14:13 "Do not let your hearts be troubled… I shall return to take you with me"

17:12 "I have kept them true to your name… not one is lost except one who chose to be"

Garden 18:1

"There was a garden, which he and his disciples entered" (Note: No prayer; no pleading; no anxiety)

Cf. 10:17 "The Father loves me, because I lay down my life in order to take it up again. No one takes it from me. I lay it down of my own free will"

Cf.12:27-28 "Now my soul is troubled. What shall I say? Father, save me from this hour? But it was for this very reason that I have come to this hour. Father, glorify your name!"

Mark	Matthew	Luke	John
Arrest 14:43-52	**Arrest 26:47-56**	**Arrest 22:47-53**	**Arrest 18:2-11**
• Judas with armed crowd sent by religious authorities identifies Jesus with a kiss • A bystander cuts off ear of high priest's slave • Jesus protests his arrest. • All forsake him and flee • Young follower runs away naked	• Jesus: "Friend, why are you here?" • One of followers cuts off ear of High Priest's slave. • Jesus' teaching: "Put sword back…" • All disciples desert him and run away	• Judas leads a crowd • He draws near to kiss Jesus • Jesus: "Judas, would you betray the Son of Man with a kiss?" • Followers ask to strike. • One of them cuts off right ear • Jesus' teaching: "No more of this…" • Jesus heals wounded man • Jesus protests his arrest	• Judas with cohort and religious officials • Knowing all, Jesus announces identity: "I am he" and they fall to ground. He permits disciples to go ("Not one is lost") • Peter cuts off right ear of Malchus • Jesus' teaching: "Am I not to drink…?"

FURTHER READING

READINGS ON GETHSEMANE

M. Israel,   *Gethsemane* (London: Collins, 1987)
J. Neyrey,   "Jesus in the Garden" in *The Passion According to Luke* (New York: Paulist, 1985) pp. 49-68
D. Stanley,   *Jesus in Gethsemane* (New York: Paulist, 1980)

READINGS ON THE PASSION AND DEATH

J. Green,   "Crucifixion" in *The Cambridge Companion to Jesus* (Cambridge: Cambridge University Press, 2001) chapter 6
D. McBride,   Characters of the passion story: Caiaphas, Pontius Pilate, Judas, and the Good Thief in *Impressions of Jesus* (Chawton: Redemptorist Publications, 2000)
                Reflections on the cross in *Seasons of the Word* (Chawton: Redemptorist Publications, 2000) pp. 96-97, 102-105, 398-399
D. Senior,   *The Passion of Jesus in the Gospel of Matthew* (Minnesota: Liturgical Press, 1990); *The Passion of Jesus in the Gospel of Mark* (Minnesota: Liturgical Press 1991); *The Passion of Jesus in the Gospel of Luke* (Minnesota: Liturgical Press 1990); *The Passion of Jesus in the Gospel of John* (Leominster: Gracewing, 1991)
J.D. Crossan,   *Who Killed Jesus?* (San Francisco: Harper, 1995)
R.E. Brown,   *The Death of the Messiah*, Vols 1 & 2 (London: Chapman, 1994)
F. Matera,   *Passion Narratives and Gospel Theologies* (New York: Paulist Press, 1986)
G. O'Collins,   "The Death of Jesus" in *Interpreting Jesus* (London: Chapman, 1983) pp. 74-105
J.P. Mackey,   "The Death of Jesus" in *Jesus, the Man and the Myth* (London: SCM, 1979) pp. 52-85
H.R. Weber,   *The Cross* (London: SPCK, 1979)
J. Moltmann,   "The Trial of Jesus" in *The Crucified God* (London: SCM, 1977) pp. 112-159

Mark

Arrest

- Jesus went to Gethsemane
- Jesus took Peter, James, John
- prayed three times
- Judas came; kissed Jesus
- Slave's ear cut off
- Jesus protested his arrest
- Young man fled naked

Before Jewish authority

- Jesus led to high priest and Peter followed
- Sanhedrin night trial
- Temple charge
- "Are you the Messiah?"
- Sentence
- Mockery of Jesus: "Prophesy"
- Peter's three denials
- Sanhedrin morning meeting
- Jesus led to Pilate

Matthew

Arrest

- Jesus went to Gethsemane
- Jesus took Peter, James, John
- prayed three times
- Judas came; kissed Jesus
- Slave's ear cut off
- Jesus protested his arrest

Before Jewish Authority

- Jesus led to Caiaphas and Peter followed
- Sanhedrin night trial
- Temple charge
- "Are you the Messiah?"
- Sentence
- Mockery of Jesus: "Prophesy"
- Peter's three denials
- Sanhedrin morning meeting
- Jesus led to Pilate

Luke

Arrest

- Jesus came to the place
- Jesus withdrew and prayed
- Judas came to kiss Jesus
- Slave's right ear cut off and healed
- Jesus protested his arrest

Before Jewish Authority

- Jesus led to high priest's house and Peter followed
- Mockery of Jesus: "Prophesy"
- Peter's three denials
- Sanhedrin morning meeting
- "Are you the Messiah?"
- Jesus led to Pilate

John

Arrest

- Jesus crossed the Kidron to a garden
- Judas came
- Soldiers and police fall
- Malchus' right ear cut off

Before Jewish authority

- Jesus led to Annas and Peter followed
- Other disciple admitted
- Peter's first denial
- High priest's interrogation
- Jesus protested his arrest
- Annas sent Jesus to Caiaphas
- Peter's two - three denials
- Jesus led to praetorium

Mark	Matthew	Luke	John
Before Roman authority	**Before Roman authority**	**Before Roman authority**	**Before Roman authority**
• King of the Jews? • Barabbas • Jesus scourged • Jesus sentenced to cross • Jesus mocked	• Death of Judas • King of the Jews? • Barabbas • Jesus scourged • Jesus sentenced to cross • Jesus mocked	• Accusations • King of the Jews? • Pilate: No crime • Jesus sent to Herod: mocked • Jesus returned to Pilate • Barabbas • Jesus delivered to them	• What accusation? • King of the Jews? • Pilate: No case • Barabbas • Jesus is scourged and mocked • "Behold the man" • Pilate challenged by Jesus • "Here is your king" • Jesus handed to them to be crucified
Cross and death	**Cross and death**	**Cross and death**	**Cross and death**
• Simon of Cyrene • Came to Golgotha (Skull) • Wine with myrrh • Crucified him • Lots for garments • Inscription over him • Robber on each side • Derided by passers-by • Mocked by priests/scribes • Reviled by co-crucified	• Simon of Cyrene • Came to Golgotha (Skull) • Wine with gall • Crucified him • Lots for garments • Inscription over him • Robber on each side • Derided by passers-by • Mocked by priests/scribes • Reviled by robbers	• Simon of Cyrene • Women of Jerusalem • Came to place called Skull • Crucified him • Criminal on each side • "Father, forgive them" • Lots for garments • People watched him • Rulers scoffed • Vinegar offered • Inscription over him • One criminal reviled • Other defended Jesus • "This day in Paradise"	• Jesus carried own cross • Came to Golgotha (Skull) • Crucified him • Another one each side • Title on the cross • Mother and three women • Mother and beloved disciple • "Behold son/mother"

PASSION NARRATIVE

Mark	Matthew	Luke	John
Cross and death	**Cross and death**	**Cross and death**	**Cross and death**
• Sixth hour darkness • Ninth hour: "Eloi, eloi, lama sabacthani" • Offer of vinegar • Jesus gave a loud cry • Breathed his last • Curtain torn • Centurion: "Son of God" • Women (four) saw from afar	• Sixth hour darkness • Ninth hour: "Eli, Eli, lama sabacthani" • Offer of vinegar • Jesus gave a loud cry • Yielded his spirit • Curtain torn • Earthquake • Dead raised and walk • Centurion: "Son of God" • Women (four) saw from afar	• Sixth hour darkness • Eclipse; curtain torn • Jesus gave a loud cry • "I commend my spirit" • Breathed his last • Centurion: "Innocent" • Bystanders repented • Women stand at a distance • All friends stand at a distance	• "I thirst" • Offer of vinegar • "It is finished" • Handed over the spirit • Jews want body removed • Soldiers pierce Jesus' side
Burial	**Burial**	**Burial**	**Burial**
• Joseph of Arimathea • Pilate checked on death • Body wrapped in shroud • Rock tomb • Stone against door • Mary Magdalene and Mary (Joset's mother)	• Joseph of Arimathea • Body wrapped in shroud • New rock tomb • Stone against door • Mary Magdalene and other Mary • Guard placed on tomb	• Joseph of Arimathea • Body wrapped in shroud • Unused rock tomb • Day of preparation • Women of Galilee prepared spices	• Joseph of Arimathea • Nicodemus • Spices and ointment • Body in cloth wrappings • Unused garden tomb • Day of preparation

Event	Jesus	Peter
place	Jesus is led off to the high priest's palace	Peter follows to the courtyard of the palace
main accuser	high priest	high priest's servant-girl
people involved	chief priests, elders and scribes	attendants and servants
pre-judgement	whole Sanhedrin looking for evidence to pass the death sentence	Peter follows Jesus; he is presumed to be a disciple
1st accusation	He said: "I have power to destroy this temple and in three days build it up"	"You were with Jesus, the man from Nazareth"
accused responds	No response, since their accusations are conflicting	Peter denies: "I do not know what you are talking about"
2nd accusation	High priest: "Have you no response to that?"	To bystanders: "This fellow is one of them"
accused responds	Jesus is silent and makes no answer	Peter denies he is "one of them"
3rd accusation	"Are you the Christ, the Son of the Blessed One?"	"You are one of them, for sure. Why, you are a Galilean!"
accused responds	Jesus confesses: "I am"	Peter denies he is "one of them"
outcome	They all give their verdict: he deserves to die	The cock crows. Peter recalls the words of Jesus and weeps
consequence	Jesus is led away to Pilate who hands him over to be crucified	Peter abandons Jesus and leaves him to his destiny
prophecy of the future	Seen to be fulfilled: "You will all lose faith. The shepherd will be struck down and the sheep will be scattered. You [Peter] will disown me three times"	Seen to be false: "If I have to die with you, I will never disown you"

Event	Peter	Beloved Disciple
Last Supper	• Not next to Jesus • Signs to beloved disciple to ask Jesus about betrayer	• Reclining next to Jesus; asks Jesus directly • Jesus replies
At the door of the high priest's palace	• Follows Jesus after arrest • Stays outside door • Is brought inside • Asked: "Are you another of the man's disciples?" • Denies discipleship to doorkeeper	• Follows Jesus after arrest • Goes with Jesus into palace • Speaks to doorkeeper • Brings Peter inside • Known to doorkeeper and other as a disciple • Does not deny
At the cross	• Absent	• At the cross he is given as son to mother of Jesus • She is given to him as mother
At the empty tomb	• Sets out with beloved disciple • They run together • Arrives second • Goes into the tomb first • Sees linen cloths	• Sets out with Peter • They run together • Arrives First • Looks in and waits for Peter • Goes into tomb after Peter • Sees and believes
In the company of the risen Jesus	• Like other disciples, fails to recognise Jesus • Questioned by Jesus: • "Do you love me more than these others do?" • "They will lead you where you do not want to go".	• Explains to Peter: "It is the Lord" • Not questioned • "If I want him to stay behind, what is that to you?"

The primacy of love in the Gospel of John is illustrated in the new mandate: "I give you a new commandment: love one another; just as I have loved you. By this love you have for one another, everyone will know that you are my disciples" (Jn 13:34-35). The beloved disciple epitomises this love; his name incorporates the fulfilment of Jesus' new commandment.

In Jesus' question to Peter ("Do you love me more than these others do?"), Peter, the figure of authority, is challenged to become the figure of love.

REFLECTION: SHOT GLASS
BY A.R. AMMONS

I'll never forget the day this beautiful woman
right out in the office said I was "sneaky":

I didn't know I was sneaky: I didn't feel
sneaky: but there are mechanisms below our

mechanisms, so I assume the lady was right:
living with that has not helped my progress

in the world, if there is such a thing,
progress, I mean: also it has hurt my image

of myself: I have used up much fellow-
feeling on the general – all of which I have

forgotten specifically about, as have the
fellows – no offices, no clear images or

demonstrations – I don't understand why that
one remark holds its place unforgivingly in me:

and now to talk about it, admit to the world
(my reading public, as it happens) that I am

scarred by an old, old wound about to heal and
about to bleed: this may do confessional good

but I will no longer appear perfect to others:
conceivably, that would be a good thing:

others may be scarred, too, but who wants to
be like them: one should: perhaps I really

do, because lonely splendour is devastatingly
shiny but basically hard and cold, marble

walls and glistening floors: one comfort,
which I am reluctant to relish, is that the

lady is now dead – surely, I am sorry about
that,
she was a person of intelligence and

discernment, which is one reason she hurt me
so bad – well, but I mean, she won't hurt

anybody else: she probably did enough good
in her life that the Lord will forgive her:

I am trying to forgive her myself: after all
She left me some room for improvement and

A sense of what to work on. . .

The Best American Poetry 2000 (New York: Scribner Poetry, 2000) pp.30–31

6 LANGUAGE AND THE PASSION

It is interesting to note the shift in the use of language from the Gospel accounts of Jesus' ministry to the story of his passion and death.

The language of the ministry
ACTIVE VERBS: **Jesus makes things happen**
During the public ministry, Jesus is presented as the protagonist whose leadership is demonstrated through the unique authority of his deeds and words, a commanding presence who gives definition to his mission by his vigorous actions and teaching. His identity, like that of every human being, is gradually revealed through his actions and words. So, for example, we learn about Jesus through his active verbs:

- Jesus teaches with authority
- he gathers chosen disciples to be with him
- he preaches the kingdom of God
- he heals the sick
- he proves himself lord of the Sabbath
- he exercises power over the demons
- he eats with tax collectors and sinners
- he feeds multitudes of people
- he prays to God as "Abba"
- he confronts and criticises the religious authorities

The language of the passion
PASSIVE VERBS: **things happen to Jesus**
The passion narrative tells a different story. One of the most frustrating things about being a victim of violence, suffering at the hands of hostile people, is that things happens to you over which you have no control. You are no longer in charge; other people make decisions and do things to you; you are left to suffer the consequences of their actions. It is interesting to watch the language of the passion story describing what happens to Jesus. It moves to the passive tense as you watch others take charge of Jesus' life. Thus:

Christ on the Cold Stone: carved limestone, Netherlands
The sculpture left, dated about 1500, portrays an exposed and vulnerable Jesus, facing the violent plans others are making around him. He is naked, wearing only a crown of thorns. Those who look at the sculpture are invited to meditate on the psychological and physical anguish of Jesus, sitting on a cold stone, momentarily withdrawn from all the violent action around him. The pose is not unlike the traditional representation of Melancholy. This particular invention of medieval piety was meant to convey the inconsolable sorrow and loneliness of Jesus: "All you who pass by the way, see if there be any sorrow like to my sorrow" (Lam 1:12).

- Jesus is ignored by his disciples in Gethsemane
- he is handed over by Judas
- he is arrested and led away
- he is abandoned by his disciples
- he is handed over to the high priest
- he is interrogated and accused falsely
- he is condemned as deserving death
- he is spat on and struck
- he is renounced by Peter
- he is led away and handed over to Pilate
- he is tried
- he is rejected in favour of Barabbas
- he is flogged
- he is mocked as a king
- he is handed over to be crucified
- he is led away by the soldiers
- he is helped by a stranger
- he is crucified
- he is derided by passers-by
- he is mocked by the chief priests
- he is taunted by the co-crucified

Power not exercised

In the language of the Gospel, you expect Jesus as the shepherd to lead and others to follow his leadership. In the passion, however, there is a dramatic shift: the time comes when the shepherd is struck down, and the sheep are scattered (see Mk 14:27). The opposite of passion is *apatheia*, a Greek word that means the inability to suffer, the condition where avoiding suffering becomes such a dominant goal that one avoids human relationships and contacts altogether. In the passion Jesus endures suffering and demonstrates a unique leadership of vulnerability. As the poet Seamus Heaney observed in this excerpt from his poem, "Weighing In:"

Kim Yong Gil:
The Crucifixion (detail)

And this is all the good tidings amount to:
This principle of bearing, bearing up
And bearing out, just having to

Balance the intolerable in others
Against our own, having to abide
Whatever we settled for and settled into

Against our better judgement. Passive
Suffering makes the world go round . . .

Prophesy who struck thee! When soldiers mocked
Blindfolded Jesus and he didn't strike back

They were neither shamed nor edified, although
Something was made manifest — the power
Of power not exercised, of hope inferred
By the powerless forever.

Seamus Heaney,
The Spirit Level
(London: Faber & Faber, 1996) p.17

That curious power, the power of power not exercised, is one that Jesus demonstrates throughout the passion narrative. The most common phrase in the passion narrative is, "he was led away and handed over…" That experience of leadership, of being led to painful places, is one that Jesus warns Peter about later, when he gives his principal disciple a teaching about the kind of leadership he will have to face:

> *"I tell you most solemnly,*
> *When you were young*
> *You put on your own belt*
> *And walked where you liked;*
> *But when you grow old*
> *You will stretch out your hands,*
> *And someone else will put a belt around you*
> *And lead you where you would rather not go."*
> **(Jn 21:18)**

That experience of being led to painful places, where one would rather not go, is one that Jesus first endures himself in the passion. He now teaches that it is not an experience peculiar to his own story, but one to be shared by those who exercise Christian leadership. In the modern world, that truth has been demonstrated by people like Dietrich Bonhoeffer and Archbishop Oscar Romero, who were both led to painful places, but whose leadership is honoured precisely for that very reason.

> *"The only violence the Gospel admits is violence to oneself. When Christ lets himself be killed, that is violence — letting oneself be killed.*
> *It is very easy to kill, especially when one has weapons, but how hard it is to let oneself be killed for love of the people."*
> **Oscar Romero,** The Violence of Love
> *(San Francisco: Harper & Row, 1998) p.152*

REFLECTION: HEDGEHOG
BY PAUL MULDOON

The snail moves like a
Hovercraft, held up by a
Rubber cushion of itself,
Sharing its secret

With the hedgehog. The hedgehog
Shares its secret with no one.
We say, Hedgehog, come out
Of yourself and we will love you.

We mean no harm. We want
Only to listen to what
You have to say. We want
Your answers to our questions.

The hedgehog gives nothing
Away, keeping itself to itself.
We wonder what a hedgehog
Has to hide, why it so distrusts.

We forget the god
Under this crown of thorns.
We forget that never again
Will a god trust in the world.

P. Muldoon, Selected Poems 1968-1983
(London: Faber & Faber, 1986) p.8

1) The first Christians spoke and preached about the resurrection long before they wrote about it. They proclaimed two basic truths: that God had raised Jesus from the dead, and that the risen Jesus appeared to a number of witnesses (1 Cor 15:3-5). The Gospels, written some forty to seventy years after the death and resurrection of Jesus, tell us what happened in different ways, but none of them attempts to describe the resurrection itself. They convert the proclamation of the early Church into narrative form, and tell stories about the empty tomb and appearances.

The accounts move over the resurrection in silence; they shift from Jesus' burial late on Good Friday to the finding of the tomb empty on Easter Sunday morning, with the women as the witnesses connecting the two events. There are no eyewitnesses to the resurrection, only witnesses to its truth. Unlike the canonical Gospels, the *Gospel of Peter* – a second-century text which has nothing to do with the apostle whose name it bears – tries to describe the resurrection directly:

Now in the night on which the Lord's day dawned, as the soldiers were keeping guard two by two in every watch, there came a great sound in the heaven, and they saw the heavens opened and two men descend, shining with a great light, and drawing near to the tomb. And the stone that had been set on the door rolled away by itself and went back to the side, and the tomb was opened and both of the young men entered it. When the soldiers saw this, they woke up the centurion and the elders (for they also were there keeping watch); and while they were telling them the things they had seen, they saw again three men come out of the tomb, and two of them sustaining the other, and a cross following after them. The two they saw had their heads reaching up to heaven, but the one they led had his head overpassing the heavens. And they heard a voice out of the heavens saying: Have you preached to those who sleep? And an answer was heard from the cross, saying: Yes. (IX.35-X.42)

**Piero della Francesca:
The Resurrection
of Christ**

5) **The evangelists go their own way when they narrate the appearance stories:**

- **Mark** associates the male disciples with Jesus' appearance in *Galilee*, but has no report of it in his narrative, which finishes at 16:8. Mark includes the angelic proclamation to the women, "He has risen; he is not here"; but the women run from the tomb and, because they are afraid, say nothing to anyone. To compensate for this abrupt or unfinished ending, other Christians added verses 9-20, to give the Gospel a sense of completion.

- **Matthew** has appearances to two women in Jerusalem, after they leave the tomb. What Mark has as promise, Matthew describes in story: the appearance to the male disciples in Galilee. From a mountain in Galilee, Jesus commissions the disciples to "preach to all nations". The place, "Galilee of the Gentiles" (Mt 4:15), is clearly important for Matthew: the Gospel that was first preached to "the lost sheep of the house of Israel" (Mt 10:6) is now extended to the Gentiles.

- **Luke,** for his own editorial purposes, keeps his story in Jerusalem. His Gospel opens in the Temple of Jerusalem and will conclude there; also he will tell the story of the beginnings of the Church from Jerusalem. Luke has an appearance to the two disciples on the road to Emmaus, a reported appearance to Peter and an appearance to the Eleven and their companions in Jerusalem. The final appearance includes the commission, "That repentance and forgiveness of sins should be preached in his name to all nations, beginning from Jerusalem" (Lk 24:47).

- **John** 20 focuses on Jerusalem. He opens with a visit to the tomb by Mary of Magdala, who, when she sees the stone rolled away, reports it to Simon Peter and the beloved disciple. When the two disciples reach the tomb, Peter sees only linen cloths whereas the beloved disciple sees and believes. He is the first to believe in the resurrection. Mary of Magdala is the first to see the risen Jesus and the first to proclaim he is risen. That same evening Jesus appears to the disciples in Jerusalem and breathes on them the Holy Spirit. Eight days later he appears again to the disciples, including Thomas.

  The appendix to John's Gospel, chapter 21, moves the drama to *Galilee*, where Jesus appears to the disciples by the Sea of Tiberias. Two stories focus on Peter – first in the miraculous catch of fish, then in the commissioning of Peter as shepherd: "Feed my sheep." Jesus' final word, however, is about the beloved disciple.

6) The resurrection narratives are written as *stories of experience* that move from the followers' disappointment and confusion, through their failure to recognise Jesus, to eventual recognition. The initial non-recognition of Jesus' close followers points to Jesus' transformation: his resurrection is not a return to his state before death, but an entrance to glory (see 1 Cor 15:35-38). Equally important, the accounts stress that the transformation does not leave behind all Jesus' own history: who he was, what he did, what he cherished, why he died – all this becomes eternally present before God. *Jesus' identity and transformation are essentially linked.*

2) The canonical Gospels make no attempt to narrate the resurrection from the point of view of eyewitnesses, but they do more than simply proclaim the truth that God raised Jesus from the dead. They move from proclamation to story.
As R.E. Brown notes:

"As vivid as these proclamations were, the story form proved to be a more effective way of conveying the full impact of the resurrection. The association between the crucifixion and the resurrection needed to be fleshed out in a dramatic way so that those who were not present in Jerusalem could understand what God had done in making Jesus victorious over death. Consequently, the Gospel stories are quite different from the brief formulas preserved for us from the early preaching."
(*Reading the Gospels with the Church*, p.66)

Ugolino di Nero:
The Deposition (detail)

3) If God's act of raising Jesus from the dead lies beyond the range of narrative expression, the evangelists do more than offer their readers summary proclamations; they offer instead two distinct stories:

a) the finding of the empty tomb
b) the appearances of the risen Jesus to his followers

These two stories put into narrative form the twofold proclamation:

a) God raised Jesus from the dead
b) We are witnesses to this

4) The women disciples of Jesus, "who, when he was in Galilee, followed him and ministered to him" (Mk 15:41), follow Jesus on the most difficult road of all, the *via dolorosa*. In the absence of Jesus' male disciples, the women provide the witness to the last hours of Jesus in Jerusalem and *provide the connection between the passion narrative and the resurrection narrative*. In Luke's Gospel the women are present for:

Passion narrative
• the way of the cross
• the crucifixion of Jesus
• the death of Jesus
• the burial of the body

Resurrection narrative
• they revisit the tomb, to anoint the body
• they find it empty
• they hear the angelic proclamation
• they return and tell the story to the apostles
• their testimony is treated as pure nonsense

7) Looking at the disciples' story of experience, we see a dramatic shift:

FROM
The disciples' destructive experience of the death of Jesus. The breakdown of discipleship in separation - loss - flight. (See John 21, where the disciples go back home and return to their former trade of fishing.) They live in the new absence of Jesus.

what happens to account for the change?

TO
The disciples' proclamation about Jesus that "God has made him both Lord and Christ, this Jesus whom you crucified" (Acts 2:36). The renewal of discipleship; refounding of the community; fearless preaching; new attachment to Jesus as Lord.

8) What happens between these two experiences to account for the change?

Clearly, there is no easy continuity between them. Just as the breakdown of discipleship was because of what happened to *Jesus*, so their conversion is dependent first on what happened to *Jesus*: "This Jesus God raised up, and of that we are all witnesses." The announcement is primarily about *what God has done to Jesus*, not about their own change. We will look at the gradual movement from the disciples' destructive experience to the beginnings of change in the story of Emmaus.

FURTHER READING

M. Bockmuehl,   "Resurrection" in *The Cambridge Companion to Jesus* (Cambridge: Cambridge University Press, 2001) chapter 7

N.T. Wright,   "The Challenge of Easter" in *The Challenge of Jesus* (London: SPCK, 2000) pp.94-113

G. Lüdemann,   "John 20: The Fourth Evangelist's Easter Stories" in *Jesus after 2000 Years* (London: SCM Press, 2000) pp.575-588

M. Barker,   *The Risen Lord: the Jesus of History as the Christ of Faith* (Edinburgh: T&T Clark, 1996)

R.E. Brown,   *Reading the Gospels with the Church* (Cincinnati: St Anthony Messenger Press, 1996)

Luke 24: 1-12: The empty tomb

Paschal witness	Human reactions
1) The empty tomb	bewilderment
2) angels' appearance (and proclamation)	fear
3) Jesus' prophetic words	recollection, memory

Story's conclusion

Paschal witness	Human reactions
4) "all this" as message to disciples and the rest	disbelief
5) empty tomb checked by Peter	amazement

Luke 24: 13-35: The road to Emmaus

Paschal witness	Human reactions
6) Jesus' presence on the road	non-recognition
7) Jesus' interpretation of scripture	burning hearts
8) Jesus breaking the bread	recognition

Story's conclusion

Paschal witness	Human reactions
9) return to tell all this	proclamation of new paschal witness by apostolic assembly
10) "The Lord has risen indeed and has appeared to Simon"	disciples tell their story

Luke 24: 36-49: The appearance to the disciples

Paschal witness	Human reactions
11) Jesus' appearance and greeting of peace	alarm and fear
12) Jesus invites disciples to see and touch him	joy but disbelief
13) Jesus eats the fish offered to him	
14) Jesus interprets scripture and commissions his disciples	their minds are opened

Luke 24:50-53: Ascension as conclusion of the Jesus story

Paschal witness	Human reactions
15) Jesus blesses them and ascends	the disciples worship him and return with great joy to Jerusalem

Thus Luke's Easter account is closed as the Gospel itself is closed with the end of the story of Jesus in the ascension; but it is not the end of the community's story. The visit of God's salvation in Jesus, heralded at the beginning of the Gospel by Zechariah (1:68-79), is now concluded with Jesus' final departure. Luke closes his Gospel as he began it, in the Temple.

8 EMMAUS: BROKEN DISCIPLESHIP RENEWED

1) The road to Emmaus is one of the famous lost roads of history. Even if we could securely identify the village, the road is missing. And it is the road we dream of, the road where we can share the burden of our disappointments, the defeat of hopes that once defined us, and be touched again by the wisdom of the compassionate stranger. The story of Emmaus appears a particularly modern one, of people journeying inside their story of separation and loss and struggling to find a language for their pain and bewilderment:

> *All that memory loves the most*
> *was once our only hope to be.*
> *And all that hope adored and lost*
> *has melted into memory.*

2) Luke is the only evangelist to explore the "inside story" of the breakdown of discipleship by introducing us to two unknown disciples and inviting us to listen to their story. We listen to their story of experience: how they knew Jesus as a prophet mighty in deed and word. We listen to their story of expectation: how they hoped Jesus would be the Messiah. We listen to their story of loss: how their hopes died with the death of Jesus. After interpreting their experience in the language of loss and disappointment, the disciples then listen to another interpretation that reaches dramatically different conclusions.

disciples' experience of the death of Jesus	➡	identity: ex-disciples of a dead prophet direction: going away from Jerusalem outlook: "our own hopes had been..."

Although the disciples are speaking about the last days of the Jesus story, they are also telling their own story: how all these "recent happenings" have affected them. They share their experience of Jesus and also the expectation that rose out of that experience.

Their experience of Jesus	Versus	Their expectation of Jesus
Jesus' deeds and words ⬇ name: prophet but put to death by chief priests and leaders		Jesus would be the one to set Israel free

3) **The disciples' story of suffering and loss**

The disciples cannot deny their experience and still hold fast to their expectations. They cannot cling to their hope in Jesus knowing what has happened to him. The death of Jesus accounts for the collapse of their hopes and the premature death of their own discipleship. It is not only that Jesus' body has gone into the tomb; their own hopes have also been buried with him. Who they were was tied to who they believed he was. Their principal identity as Jesus' disciples has been shattered because of what happened to him.

4) **The Jesus story of suffering and glory**

The risen Jesus, still a stranger, re-interprets their experience of recent events in the light of scripture. It is a story that tries to make sense of pain and rejection and brokenness. Again Luke uses a familiar theme: moving away from an exclusive inspection of the details of present experience to put the story into the context of the larger story of prophecy. This is always done in the belief that the larger frame can help to understand the immediate frame of the new experience.

New Experience or Story

PROPHECY
(old story)

New Interpretation

5) **The movement to table**

The talking on the road now moves to silent revelation at the table. In the breaking of the bread the stranger gives himself away, literally, in the bread. In table fellowship, which has been a distinguishing mark of Jesus' ministry, the disciples are enabled to see the stranger as the Lord. In this new experience of grace they can reinterpret the past and face the future.

Immediately, they make the journey towards the place they had reason to leave, Jerusalem. Their colloquium on the road and the table fellowship help them to see the "recent happenings" in a new light. When they arrive, their story is offered to the Eleven and the others as a confirmation of the Lord's appearance to Simon.

George Tooker:

Supper

disciples' experience of the risen Lord		identity: disciples of the risen Lord
		direction: hurrying towards Jerusalem
		outlook: new story of experience

6) The structure of the Emmaus story gives the Christian community a perfect reminder of coming to know Jesus as Lord in the Eucharist:

the coming together
the hearing of the story
the gathering around the table
the breaking of the bread
the recognition of Jesus as Lord
the renewal of personal discipleship
the departure to share the good news.

FURTHER READING

D. McBride,   *Emmaus: the Gracious Visit of God According to Luke* (Dublin: Dominican Publications, 1997) pp. 121-160; "Mary, the wife of Cleopas" in *Impressions of Jesus*

REFLECTION: THE GRAVEYARD OF HOPES

We had hoped...
that our loved ones would not be taken from us;
that things would get easier;
that every hurt would be balanced by joy;
that God would become clearer somehow;
that peace would be secured among peoples;
that comedy would triumph;
that justice would be established;
that our good health would endure;
that people would become kinder;

that racism would be unknown;
that every religion would be esteemed;
that tragedy would happen only onstage;
that wrinkles would appear only on our clothing;
that we could lay down our burdens;
that we could forsake our sins;
that we would not be forgotten;
that...
So it goes on and on and on,
making for the largest cemetery in the world.

Event	Luke 24:49-53	Acts 1:1-14
Luke's purpose	Luke concludes his Gospel with Jesus' victory over death and his return in glory to the Father. Jesus leaves behind him an unfinished community that is powerless to reorganise itself for mission: they must wait for God's gift. Jesus' return to God completes his earthly ministry.	Luke opens the story of the Church by building a bridge back to the Gospel. Jesus crosses the bridge to instruct the Twelve about the kingdom of God and commission them. They are to wait in Jerusalem for the promise of the Father. Jesus' return to God marks the beginning of the Church's life.
Place of ascension	Bethany (on Mount of Olives)	Mount of Olives
Time	Easter Sunday evening	40 days after the passion
The final instructions of Jesus	i) Mission: Repentance preached to all the nations, beginning in Jerusalem. ii) But: "Stay in the city until you are clothed with power from on high."	i) Not for disciples to know the date of the end of the world. ii) Mission: When they receive the Spirit, they must then witness not only in Jerusalem, but throughout Judea, Samaria, and to the ends of the earth.
Jesus' departure	After blessing them, Jesus withdraws from them and is carried up to heaven.	He is lifted up while they look on, and a cloud takes him from their sight.
Disciples' reaction	i) After worshipping him, they return to Jerusalem full of joy. ii) They are continually in the Temple praising God.	i) They continue staring into the sky. ii) They are questioned about this by two men in white who announce that Jesus will come back in the same way as they saw him go. iii) They return to Jerusalem, to the upper room. Three groups make up the principal witnesses from the Gospel: the eleven apostles; the women of Galilee; Mary and the brothers of Jesus. This community of Gospel memory join together in prayer. They wait for God to make them a community of Spirit.

Luke has two narratives of the ascension. The Gospel narrative serves as a majestic conclusion to the story of Jesus who now returns, his mission completed, to the fullness of God. Luke is not going to tell the story of the beginnings of the Church without Jesus, so he shows Jesus present to the community at the beginning of this new story of salvation.

As Luke had characters cross the bridge from the Old Testament to meet Mary and Jesus in his infancy narrative, so in this transitional chapter in Acts he has Jesus cross the bridge from the Gospel to meet and commission the founding Twelve of the new community. Thus Luke dramatises how the new community is founded in personal attachment to the person of Jesus and his teaching, and in the gift of the Holy Spirit at Pentecost.

10 ESTABLISHING AN APOSTOLIC COMMUNITY OF MEMORY & SPIRIT

The end of the Gospel: Luke 24:36-53

1) Jesus appears to the assembled disciples, offering them peace. The new community will be founded in reconciliation. They cannot believe, however, that it is he. Since their eyes fail them, Jesus appeals to their sense of touch. Again, Luke underlines that the appearance of the risen Jesus by itself does *not* make for Easter faith. Something more is needed.

2) Jesus then appeals to their memory: he interprets the meaning of what he said during the ministry, and *opens their minds* to understand the scriptures, uncovering their mission to preach to all the nations.

3) He gives them a mission statement, but does not send them on mission; instead, he tells them to stay in the city until something happens to them: they will be clothed with the power from on high.

4) He departs, leaving behind him **an unfinished community.** The ascension, on Easter Sunday evening, marks the fulfilment of Jesus' mission and the conclusion of the Gospel.

The beginning of the Acts: 1:1-2:4

5) **Beginning with the risen Jesus**
Luke is not going to begin the story of the Church in the absence of Jesus. The beginning of Acts *shows* the truth that the Church is rooted in attachment to Jesus and founded in his authoritative word. Hence the forty days of teaching.

6) **The mission to the world and the departure of Jesus**
In the final words of Jesus, Luke clarifies two important issues: a) the outpouring of the Spirit does not signal the parousia; b) salvation is not limited to Israel but extended to the ends of the earth. With these questions settled, Jesus is lifted up.

7) **The community of memory**
Three groups are assembled: the eleven apostles; the women of Galilee; Mary, the mother of Jesus, and his brothers. These three groups of witnesses cross the bridge and bring Luke's Gospel in its entirety into the beginning of Acts. They form the basic community of memory, the witnesses of Jesus' full story.

8) **Beginning with the Twelve**
Luke is not going to begin the Church with eleven apostles; the New Israel must begin with twelve. To be numbered among the twelve, the new candidate must belong to the community of memory – from the time of John's baptism to the ascension (1:21).

9) **The community of Spirit**
The community of memory can function as *witnesses* only when they become a community of Spirit. The outpouring of the Spirit at Pentecost enables the community to testify not only to Jesus' life, death and resurrection, but to the *significance* of all that this means now.

10) Luke's carefully drawn portrait of **the Church as a community of memory and Spirit** is one of his great gifts to us. The Church is a community forever identified with a dangerous memory of Jesus: it is a Church that lives *ex memoria passionis, mortis et resurrectionis Jesu.* That memory of Jesus - who he was, what he did and said, his values and preferences, his death and resurrection - all this gives the community its roots and direction.

After the consecration, each Eucharistic Prayer celebrates the Christian community as a community of memory: "Father, we celebrate the *memory* of Christ, your Son. We, your people and your ministers, recall…" (Eucharistic Prayer 1). The canon ends by celebrating the congregation as a community of Spirit: "Through him, with him, in him, in the unity of the Holy Spirit…"

George Tooker:
Embrace of Peace 1

FURTHER READING

D. McBride,   "From experience to message" in *Emmaus* pp. 163-201
               Reflections on the ascension pp. 146-151;
               on Pentecost pp.158ff in *Seasons of the Word*

G. Theissen   "The Risen Jesus: Easter and its Interpretations" in
and A. Merz,   *The Historical Jesus* (London: SCM Press, 1998) pp.474-511

J. Shea,   *An Experience Named Spirit* (Chicago: Thomas More, 1983) pp. 15-52

P.L. Maier,   *First Christians* (London: Mowbrays, 1976) pp. 11-24

memory ⬅ ➡ spirit

Jesus))))))))))))))) ⬅ **us** ➡

11) Luke has a vision of the Christian community as one that is linked *back* through memory and community to the person of Jesus. Luke sees the Church as a community that is vibrantly linked through a chain of people and faith back through the apostles to the person of Jesus; it is a community that always gathers in the name of Jesus, not its own name. The *ecclesia* must be grounded in personal attachment to Jesus and his values: without the memory of Jesus the community makes itself master.

12) But the Church is more than memory, for it lives in the faith of the living Lord. It does more than look to the past; it is *a community of the Spirit of Jesus* that faces the present and looks to the future. Without the memory of Jesus, the community can invent its own values and become historically disconnected from Jesus (see Mt 7:21-23.). Without the Spirit, the community can be reduced to a group of museum attendants guarding a lifeless treasure. Not all the answers will be discovered by consulting the memory of Jesus, because Jesus did not leave an answer to everything. The future is shown by discovery, not by blueprint. When the community has a problem, they don't always say: "Jesus said this." Rather, they say: "It has been decided by the Spirit and by us" (Acts 15:28). Thus the Church has the ability to discover its future through the issues it encounters and God's accompanying grace.

13) According to Luke's portrait, the Church has to be a community of memory and Spirit, keeping these two in creative tension. St Bernard made the same point when he spoke of the Church as *"ecclesia ante et retro occulata"* – the Church that must have eyes for what is ahead and for what is past. The Church preaches the Gospel to the world it is sent to, and keeps alive the sacred memory of the one who initiated this life, Jesus of Nazareth. Each generation is connected to the previous one and the next one; each generation receives the message and passes it on.

REFLECTION: THREE POEMS

That act of passing on is essential to the life of the community – the alternative is people living in the past, a state described eloquently by Philip Larkin in his poem, "The Old Fools:"

Perhaps being old is having lighted rooms
Inside your head, and people in them, acting.
People you know, yet can't quite name: each looms
Like a deep loss restored, from known doors turning,
Setting down a lamp, smiling from a stair, extracting
A known book from the shelves; or sometimes only
The rooms themselves, chairs and a fire burning,
The blown bush at the window, or the sun's
Faint friendliness on the wall some lonely
Rain-ceased midsummer evening. That is where they live:
Not here and now, but where all happened once.

P. Larkin, *High Windows*
(London: Faber & Faber, 1974) pp.19,20

A more positive image of someone spending a life handing on the tradition is explored in R. S. Thomas' poem "The Country Clergy":

I see them working in old rectories
By the sun's light, by candlelight,
Venerable men, their black cloth
A little dusty, a little green
With holy mildew. And yet their skulls,
Ripening over so many prayers,
Toppled into the same grave
With oafs and yokels. They left no books,
Memorial to their lonely thought
In grey parishes; rather they wrote
On men's hearts and in the minds
Of young children sublime words
Too soon forgotten. God in his time
Or out of time will correct this.

R.S. Thomas, *Collected Poems 1945-1990* (London: Phoenix, 1996) p.82

In "God's Grandeur" Gerard Manley Hopkins celebrates the attentive power of the Spirit: that for all the "smudge" we make on our world, there lives "the dearest freshness deep down things":

The world is charged with the grandeur of God.
It will flame out, like shining from shook foil;
It gathers to a greatness, like the ooze of oil
Crushed. Why do men then now not reck his rod?
Generations have trod, have trod, have trod;
And all is seared with trade; bleared, smeared with toil;
And wears man's smudge and shares man's smell: the soil
Is bare now, nor can foot feel, being shod.

And for all this, nature is never spent;
There lives the dearest freshness deep down things;
And though the last lights off the black West went
Oh, morning, at the brown brink eastward, springs—
Because the Holy Ghost over the bent
World broods with warm breast and with ah! bright wings.

W.H. Gardner, *Gerard Manley Hopkins: Poems and Prose* (Harmondsworth: Penguin Books, 1963) p.27

11

RECOGNISING PAUL'S CONTRIBUTION

1) Before saying something about Paul, it might be useful to look at the various groups mentioned in the Acts. Jesus himself, his apostles and early followers originally belonged to the first group: they were **Jews** who believed in the one God, the God of Israel and the God of their ancestors. They followed the Law, worshipped in the Temple, kept the great feasts, and accepted the "scriptures" – the sacred writings we call the Old Testament or the Hebrew scriptures. Acts represents the Jerusalem community as sharing in the daily Temple cult, while meeting in private homes for common meals and prayer (2:42, 46). These are the **Hebrew Christians**, although they were not called Christians, but were referred to as a Jewish sect, "the sect of the Nazarenes" (24:5) – comparable to "the sect of the Pharisees" (15:5) or the "sect of the Sadducees" (5:17). The Hebrew Christians spoke Aramaic and followed the requirements of the Jewish Law.

The early Christians:
Groupings at the beginning of the Church

2) The Hellenists were Jews who preferred to use the Greek language in worship and scripture. They were non-Palestinian Jews, who came from a wide variety of places in the Diaspora, who had settled in Jerusalem, and had their own meeting in their own language. Some of them became Christians, forming parallel worshipping communities to the Hebrew Christians. The **Hellenist Christians** were much more radical than their Hebrew counterparts: they called for the abolition of Temple worship and the revision of the Law of Moses, because Jesus superseded Moses.

3) In Acts 6:1 there is tension in the Christian community in Jerusalem: *the Hellenists complain that their widows are being overlooked.* The Twelve call a full meeting of the disciples and tell the Hellenists to select their own leaders, "seven men of good reputation". Stephen is elected as their leader, alongside six others, including Philip. Soon after Stephen starts preaching, and he is arrested and brought before the Sanhedrin. After Stephen's execution there is a persecution of Hellenist Christians (8:1). This does not affect the apostles, who are Hebrew Christians, and they remain safely in Jerusalem. Philip starts preaching in Samaria, and is so successful that Peter and John go up to baptise the new converts (8:17). The Hellenists are forced to go beyond the circle of local Jews, paving the way for the mission to the Gentiles, and the birth of the **Gentile Christians.**

Jews — Hebrew Christians — Hellenist Christians — Gentile Christians

4) Philip is inspired to take the Gentile road – the road that leads from Jerusalem to Gaza, one of the Gentile cities on the coastal plain (8:26). He meets a eunuch, the chief treasurer of the queen of Ethiopia. Philip opens the scriptures to him and then baptises the African convert. Philip moves on to another Gentile city, Caesarea on the coast, to continue his preaching. *Before Peter goes to Caesarea, Philip is preaching there.*

5) The full development of the mission to the Gentiles is connected with Paul. He was born in Tarsus, in the Greek-speaking Diaspora, the son of a Palestinian Jew. According to Luke, he was educated in Jerusalem at the school of Gamaliel (Acts 22:3). Paul belongs to two worlds, something he has in common with the Hellenists. His spiritual home in Jerusalem would have been the Greek-speaking synagogues.

6) It is difficult to exaggerate the role and influence of Paul in the formation of the Christian Church. Although Luke's second volume is entitled *Acts of the Apostles*, about 60% of the writing is devoted to Paul. Half the books in the New Testament, all pre-dating the written Gospels, are Paul's letters to the new convert communities in the Mediterranean world. Two of the evangelists, Mark and Luke, are traditionally understood to have been Paul's companions.

7) **The story of Paul's conversion**
According to his own writing (Gal 1:1, 11-16; 1 Cor 9:1, 15:8; Phil 3:5-6) the greatest change in Paul's thinking was brought about as a consequence of his vision of Christ on the road to Damascus. In this vision Christ commissioned him to preach to the Gentiles. According to Luke's three accounts in Acts (9:1-19; 22:1-16; 26:9-18) Ananias mediated Paul's commission to him.

Saul		Paul
(Hebrew Name)		*(Graeco-Roman Name)*
Hebrew born of Hebrews Pharisee… faultless persecutor of the Church (Phil 3:5-6)	*identity*	**Apostle appointed by God Servant of Christ, who works harder than others (2 Cor 11:23)**
Hunter of the followers of the way (Acts 9:2)	*direction*	**Travelling preacher to the Gentiles (Gal 2:9)**
"My enthusiasm was for the tradition of my ancestors" (Gal 1:14)	*outlook*	**"All I want is to know Christ and the power of his resurrection" (Phil 3:10)**

"Paul's conversion convinced him of three facts: that Christ was alive, that in some way the risen Christ was to be identified with the disciples whom Paul had persecuted, and that in this revelation of Christ God was commissioning him for a great new enterprise. These facts changed completely his attitude to Christ, to Christians, and to himself, and with characteristic thoroughness he started to think through the implications and reconstruct around them the edifice of his religious belief.

How long this reconstruction took we can only guess, because the evidence is all contained in epistles written from fifteen to thirty years later. No doubt Paul continued to grow in spiritual wisdom throughout his lifetime, and we know that what he learnt from personal experience was later enriched by the traditions he received from the church."

(G.B. Caird, The Apostolic Age, *p. 120)*

9) **Looking at decisive moments**

a) **Paul's early struggle in Jerusalem (Acts 9:26ff)** Luke's account of how Paul fails to be accepted by the disciples in Jerusalem.

b) **Paul and Barnabas in Antioch (Acts 11:22f; 15:1ff.)** The three-year mission of Paul and Barnabas in the third greatest city in the world.

c) **Paul at Jerusalem (Acts 15:5ff; Gal 2)** Looking at the accounts of the apostolic council in Jerusalem, 49 AD.

d) **His relationship with Peter and James**

e) **Paul's unique place in the early Church** The sum of his theology and personality.

f) **Paul's recognition as 'apostle' in Roman Canon**

The second-century Roman writer Onesiphoros gives a description of Paul in his work, Acts of Paul and Thecla. *Paul, he writes, is "rather small in size, bald-headed, bow-legged, with eyebrows that met, and with a large, red and rather hooked nose. Strongly built, he was full of grace, for at times he looked like a man, at times like an angel."*

Fresco of Paul:
13ᵗʰ Century

FURTHER READING

J.D.G. Dunn,   *The Theology of Paul the Apostle* (Edinburgh: T&T Clark, 1998)

C.K. Barrett,   *Paul: An Introduction to his Thought* (London: Chapman, 1994)

M. Goulder,   *A Tale of Two Missions* (London: SCM, 1994)

S. Brown,   *The Origins of Christianity* (Oxford: University Press, 1993) pp. 101-128

D. McBride,   Reflections on Paul in *Seasons of the Word* pp. 136-139; 144-145; 380-383

G. Lüdemann,   *Opposition to Paul in Jewish Christianity* (Minneapolis: Fortress, 1989)

G.B. Caird,   *The Apostolic Age* (London: Duckworth, 1966) pp. 116-140

HOW THE GOSPELS DEVELOPED BACKWARDS

1) The original Gospel heralded by Jesus was a spoken word. Jesus was a voice, not a penman; he was a preacher, not a scribe. He used direct speech and deeds of power (what we call miracles) to communicate his message. In the apostolic proclamation there is a dramatic shift from Jesus the preacher to Jesus the preached, concentrating on what pertained to Jesus' proclamation about God.

The oldest Christian preaching about Jesus concerned his death and resurrection, and the earliest writing in the New Testament (the letters of Paul) focused on the same central theme. Given that the events surrounding Jesus' death were the central focus of the whole public ministry, the early preachers were bound to have first formed a standardised sequence of the last days of Jesus for their hearers.

Their claims about the identity and mission of Jesus rested, above all, on an interpretation of what happened during his last days. Since their first listeners were all Jews, this interpretation also needed to show how these events corresponded with scriptural prophecy. This sequence can be seen in the formula Paul uses in 1 Corinthians 15:3-4:

- *Jesus' identity asserted:* "Christ"
- *his mission interpreted:* "died for our sins… was raised on the third day"
- *consistent with prophecy:* "in accordance with the scriptures"

The evangelists developed the proclamation of Jesus' death and resurrection by prefixing the ministry material to the passion accounts.

2) To help us understand the development of the Gospels, the Church has given us a helpful guide, *Instruction on the Historical Truth of the Gospels,* which was produced by the Pontifical Biblical Commission in 1964; its substance was incorporated into Vatican II's Constitution on Divine Revelation in 1965. The document tells us: "To judge properly concerning the reliability of what is transmitted in the Gospels, the interpreter should pay diligent attention to the three stages of tradition by which the doctrine and the life of Jesus have come down to us" (VI, 2). The three stages of tradition are:

Stage 1: **The public ministry of Jesus of Nazareth:** What Jesus did and said during the public ministry that was witnessed by his chosen followers

Stage 2: **The apostolic preaching about Jesus:** What the apostles preached about Jesus in the light of his resurrection from the dead

Stage 3: **The evangelists' written Gospels:** What the "sacred authors" committed to writing, "taken from the many things handed down".

Stage 1: The public ministry of Jesus
(c. AD 30-33)

The Commission limits the first stage of the tradition to the public ministry, excluding from consideration Jesus' infancy and early years. When the Commission refers to "the beginning" it specifies the moment Jesus "joined to himself chosen disciples" (VII). Even considering the public ministry, the Commission makes no claim that what we have in the Gospels is an exact record of that time.

We have no resources available to us that were written at the time of Jesus' ministry: the only words written about Jesus during his lifetime were those ordered to be written by Pontius Pilate. The public ministry of Jesus lasted two or three years, and traditionally we have referred to the major part of his lifetime as *the hidden years*. That acknowledgement warns us how much we do *not* know about Jesus.

Jesus lived as a Galilean Jew in the first third of the first century, a relatively peaceful period under the Roman occupation. He spent most of his life as a minor artisan, someone who worked with his hands, living in the small hill village of Nazareth. ***These years are not only unknown to us but also unknowable.***

For the last three years of his life, however, much of what Jesus did and said was available to the public, especially to his disciples who travelled with him around Galilee, Judea and elsewhere. What Jesus did and said, including the ways he chose to express himself, would help his followers to be witnesses of his public life and teaching. Many of the details of ordinary existence – about what Jesus looked like, how he remembered his own upbringing etc. – are not included as they would normally be in a biography.

Stage 2: The apostolic preaching about Jesus
(c. AD 33-70)

The second stage of the tradition refers to what the apostles and disciples preached about

Jesus after the first Easter. As the Commission says, the content of their proclamation was ***"above all the death and resurrection of the Lord, as they bore witness to Jesus"*** (VII). Examples of this can be seen in 1 Corinthians 15:3-4; Acts 2:23-32; 3:14-15; 10:39-40. The earliest preached Gospel began where our written Gospels finish - which is why we can say that the written Gospels developed backwards. As a result of their Easter experience and their enlightenment in the Spirit, the early preachers came to a fuller understanding of who Jesus was (see Jn 2:22). Their new experiences enabled them to reinterpret the past and bring it up to date.

The Four Evangelists:
(Book of Kells, Folio 27v)

The apostolic preachers who followed Jesus during his public ministry were in a unique position to witness to the fundamental continuity between Jesus of Nazareth and Jesus the risen Lord.

The preachers did not just chronicle what Jesus did and said, but "interpreted his words and deeds according to the needs of their listeners", using "catecheses, stories, testimonia, hymns, doxologies, prayers, and other literary forms of this sort" (VIII). Already, in this pre-literary stage, oral tradition was recasting stories about Jesus according to various needs, for by this time the Gospel was being preached in different languages and in different contexts (e.g. Antioch, Corinth, Ephesus, Rome).

Stage 3: The evangelists' written Gospels
(c. AD 70-100)
The stories and sayings about Jesus' passion and ministry that circulated in Stage 2, which were already modified in the light of an Easter faith, provided the evangelists' source material. Sections of that tradition, such as an outline passion narrative and brief collections of material relating to different subjects, were probably already in writing before the evangelists composed their own accounts. The Commission states that the evangelists wrote, "for the benefit of the Churches, with a method suited to the peculiar purpose which each one set for himself. From the many things handed down, they selected some things, reduced others to a synthesis, (still) others they explicated as they kept in mind the situation of the Churches" (IX).

The Commission is silent about the identity of the evangelists and makes no claims that any of them was an apostle-eyewitness. Given the Commission's statement that the evangelists' source material was handed down from Stage 2, J. Fitzmyer comments on the text: "This means, then, that none of the evangelists was an eyewitness of Jesus' ministry. They heard about Jesus and his ministry from others who were 'eyewitnesses' and who had become

The Four Evangelists:
(Detail Book of Kells, Folio 27v)

The early preachers then turned their attention to *the deeds and words of Jesus*, and thus collections of sayings, parables, and miracles grew. This attention to the ministry of Jesus would have been particularly useful for new converts who wanted to know about the earthly life and teaching of the one they professed as Lord. More importantly, attention to the ministry of Jesus would save the event of death and resurrection from evaporating into mythology.

The death and resurrection are inseparably attached to Jesus, the one who came from Nazareth, called named disciples, preached the kingdom of God in Galilee and Judea, healed the sick and disabled, told parables, challenged people to think and act differently. Rooting the significance of Jesus in the particular world of time and place was essential to a historical proclamation.

Although the testimony of the preachers was suffused with faith in Jesus as Lord, as the Commission states: "their faith rested on the things Jesus did and taught" (VIII).

'ministers of the word' (Lk 1:2)" (*Christological Catechism*, pp.25).

R.E. Brown makes a similar point: **"The wide recognition that the evangelists were not eyewitnesses of Jesus' ministry is important for understanding the differences in the Gospels. In the older approach wherein eyewitness testimony was directly involved, it was very difficult to explain differences in the Gospels... The evangelists, who were not eyewitnesses, had a task that the preachers of Stage Two never had, namely, to shape a sequential narrative from Jesus' baptism to his resurrection"** (*Reading the Gospels with the Church* pp.16,17). Matthew and Luke add the infancy narratives. They are a later development prefixed to the main body of the Gospel material, with the same message: Jesus is the Son of God. The birth of Jesus is *now* seen in the same salvific light as his death and resurrection.

Conclusion

What is important is the Commission's acknowledgement of the threefold process of Gospel formation. The Gospels are not Stage 1 documents: they are not a record of the deeds and words of Jesus from the first stage of the tradition. Neither are they Stage 2 documents: they are not examples of Gospel preaching by those who had direct experience of Stage 1. The evangelists are *authors* of Stage 3 documents. While they were faithful to the tradition they received from the intervening generation, clearly the evangelists compiled their own narratives about Jesus. The recognition of the consequences of human authorship is repeated in the 1993 document from the Biblical Commission when it writes about all biblical authors as people "who employed both their own capacities for expression and the means which their age and social context put at their disposal".

FURTHER READING

Above notes taken from D. McBride, "How the Gospels developed backwards" in *The Gospel of Mark: a Reflective Commentary* (Dublin: Dominican Publications, 1996)

The Pontifical Biblical Commission,	*The Interpretation of the Bible in the Church* (Rome: Libreria Editrice Vaticana, 1993); *The Historical Truth of the Gospels* (Rome, 1964)
J. Fitzmyer,	*A Christological Catechism: New Testament Answers* (New York: Paulist, 1991)
H. Hendrickx,	*From One Jesus to Four Gospels* (Quezon City: Claretian, 1991) pp. 3-55

THE DEVELOPMENT OF EARLY CHRISTOLOGY

When was the mystery of Jesus' identity revealed?

1) There is a development between the way Jesus presented himself in his public ministry and the way in which his followers presented him after the Easter event. In the long tradition of Israel, no one had ever been raised from death to eternal life and glory. This claim about Jesus changed everything. The resurrection was interpreted by the believing community as a dramatic victory over death, an intervention by God that vindicated the origin of the authority that Jesus claimed and revealed. Those followers who met the risen Jesus came to realise that he was much more than they had previously understood during the public ministry.

2) How are the followers of Jesus going to communicate their new belief in him? How are they going to express their Christology? When they speak/write about Jesus, which scenes in the life of Jesus are going to become vehicles for the expression of their new faith? Scholars refer to the *Christological moment*, meaning the event in the story of Jesus that the preacher or evangelist chooses as his particular scene to communicate to his hearer/reader the truth of Jesus' identity. Will it be

- the conception and birth of Jesus?
- the youth of Jesus?
- the baptism of Jesus?
- his death and resurrection?

The first preachers (c. AD 33-70)
resurrection

Through the resurrection and the gift of the Spirit, Jesus' first followers came to believe what they could not have known before: that Jesus was the Messiah and Son of God. In the earliest preaching, the *resurrection* was the chief moment associated with the revelation of Jesus' identity. Note the following texts:

- "This Jesus God raised up... God has made him both Lord and Messiah, this Jesus whom you crucified." (Acts 2:32, 36)

- "What God promised to the fathers he has fulfilled for us their children by raising Jesus, as it is written in the second psalm: 'You are my son; today I have begotten you.'" (Acts 13:32–33)

- "Born of the seed of David according to the flesh... in the order of the Spirit he was proclaimed Son of God in all his power through his resurrection from the dead." (Rom 1:3-4)

- "Jesus became obedient unto death, even death on a cross. Therefore God has highly exalted him and bestowed on him the name [i.e. 'Lord'] which is above every name." (Phil 2:8-9)

This revelation was associated with:

1) a divine proclamation
2) the identity announced: God's Son
3) the agency of the Holy Spirit

The Gospel of Mark (c. AD 70)
baptism

By the time the first Gospel is written, a more developed Christology is dominant. Jesus is seen as Messiah and Son of God during his ministry. Mark announces Jesus' identity to the reader at the baptism, but he preserves the older understanding that this was not known until *after* the death of Jesus. So, the first human witness to understand the mystery of Jesus is the centurion: "Truly this was a son of God" (15:39). In announcing *to the readers* the identity of Jesus at his baptism, Mark preserves the older tradition that this is associated with:

1) a divine proclamation
2) the identity announced: God's Son
3) the agency of the Holy Spirit

The Gospels of Matthew and Luke (c. AD 80-85)
conception

Both Matthew and Luke press back the announcement of Jesus' identity to his conception and birth. The ideas that early Christian preaching had applied to the resurrection are now announced in the angel's message to Mary (Luke) and to Joseph (Matthew):

1) a divine proclamation
2) the identity announced: God's Son
3) the agency of the Holy Spirit

The revelation of Jesus' identity is further announced to the shepherds (Luke) and to the Magi (Matthew).

The mystery that was originally revealed in the resurrection now begins, particularly in Matthew, to become evident during the ministry to the disciples. Matthew alters Mark and has confessions of Jesus as God's Son where Mark has none (compare Mt 14:33 with Mk 6:51-52; and Mt 16:16 with Mk 8:29).

The Gospel of John (c AD 100)
pre-existence

John is alone among the evangelists in pressing back the announcement of Jesus' identity to pre-existence: "In the beginning was the Word; the Word was with God and the Word was God." In the light of his belief in who Jesus is, John rewrites Genesis. He rewrites the past of the world in order to catch with the new insight into who Jesus is as the creator of all and the ancestor of all.

John is the only evangelist to speak of the incarnation: "The Word was made flesh, he lived among us." This highly developed Christology of pre-existence and the incarnation is where most Christians begin to articulate their faith in Jesus. In the end of the Gospel tradition is the beginning of most Christians' understanding of Jesus.

FURTHER READING

S. Barton,	"Many Gospels, one Jesus?" in *The Cambridge Companion to Jesus* (Cambridge: Cambridge University Press, 2001) chapter 11
P. Frederiksen,	*From Jesus to Christ* (New Haven: Yale University Press, 2000) pp.133–176
S.M. Wylen,	*The Jews in the Time of Jesus* (New York: Paulist, 1996) pp.162–183
R.E. Brown,	*An Introduction to New Testament Christology* (London: Chapman, 1994) pp. 103–152

BRINGING THE PAST UP TO DATE

1) As you can see from the development of early Christology, faith makes a journey backwards with the light of the resurrection and reinterprets not only the past of Jesus but also the past of the world. For the apostolic community who travelled around with Jesus during the ministry, the resurrection gives significance to events and stories that seemed puzzling; it opens up a whole range of meaning that was previously closed. *"When therefore he was raised from the dead his disciples remembered that he had said this; and they believed the scriptures and the word which Jesus had spoken"* (Jn 2:22). Faith penetrates the mystery of the historical Jesus and shapes all the Gospel stories. It is the risen Jesus who interprets the meaning of the historical Jesus.

2) The death and resurrection are not events added on to the ministry; they condition the whole telling of the story. The Gospel does not lead up to the resurrection; it is born out of it. The Gospel begins with "alleluia" because it is a proclamation of the continuing presence of Jesus in the community. That is why every verse can be called Good News. *It is Easter, therefore, which makes Christmas, not vice versa.* The birth of Jesus becomes important because of his death and resurrection.

- *Examples of birth stories that are written long after the original event.* They are written in the light of new knowledge of who the person has turned out to be. When people read those stories years later, information that originally came to light only gradually is now offered at the beginning of the story. Thus the new reader is wiser than the original participants in the events.

- *Examples from literature and films of how an ending is offered at the beginning of the story,* thus altering our perception of the whole process of the story. When we already know the ending of a story, it obviously influences the way we watch and interpret the whole *development* of the story.

3) **Bringing the past up to date**
The process of *reinterpreting the past in the light of new experience* is not confined to the Gospel; it is something we do all the time.

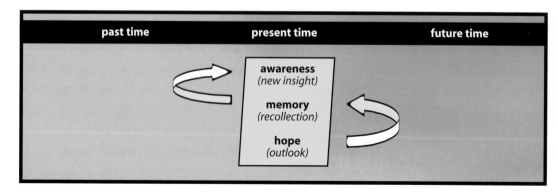

what takes place	and	what is going on
experience		meaning
fact		interpretation
event		significance
"seeing and hearing"		"perceiving and understanding"
eyewitness to event		witness to meaning

4) We bring time to mind through our awareness of the present, our memory of the past, and our hope in the future. We can also choose to ignore the present, forget the past, and despair of the future. Although memory refers to the past and hope to the future, we remember and hope *from where we are now*. The present is significant as the dividing line between the past and the future. Memory and hope are present realities. Because of new experiences and new insight, the past can be reinterpreted and understood anew. So, too, with the future. In the Old Testament, the memory of God's deed in liberating his people from Egypt always gives Israel ground to hope in the future. The people eat the memory at Passover; they feed on it; it nourishes their spirit and their hope. The same becomes true for Christians in the celebration of the eucharist: "Christ **has** died; Christ is risen; Christ *will* come again."

5) New awareness and new revelation can change the way we interpret the past.

6) Some stories only become true later, because only later does the true *significance* of the story emerge. There is a difference between what takes place and what is going on.

More often than not, the meaning of an experience is not given at the time of the experience. Some experiences have to wait for meaning; the "whole story" can never be told until both experience and meaning are put together. **Example** - the disciples in Emmaus.

Conclusion

- Stories of the past are retold in the light of new experiences.
- Memory is recreated to catch up with new awareness and new insight.
- Out of the new experience of resurrection faith, out of the love for who the Lord is now, the story of Jesus is proclaimed in word and writing.

FURTHER READING

D. McBride,   "Reinterpretation: bringing the past up to date" in *Emmaus* pp. 111-115
                 "The unity of time in the human story" in *The Month* 240 (1979) pp. 229-232

E. Schillebeeckx, "The authority of new experiences" in *Christ: the Christian Experience in the Modern World* (London: SCM, 1980) pp. 19-64

REFLECTION: BRINGING TIME TO MIND

Writing your own story would involve you in a process of bringing time to mind. You would start by recalling in as much detail as possible your past. As you began to put your past life into words, you would probably find that the story could be told in many different ways, depending on the kind of future you thought it was leading to. This would start you thinking about the possible relationships between your past and your future.

You would not be able to foresee the events of the future, nor even to recall the entirety of the past, but you would have begun to think about your life as a whole. You would think of all the elements of the drama in it: the plot, the characters, the thought content, the setting. Thinking this way would carry you to the edge of your life, backward to birth and forward to death; it would give you a sense of your lifetime being part of a larger time.

It would make you wonder how your life fits into your times, whether it is a re-enactment of some typical modern life story. You might wonder how far your story is simply the perennial human story, the everlasting cycle of childhood, youth, adulthood and age, how far it is the modern story and how far it is strictly your own story.

Composing a personal creed would set you searching for something in memory. The object of your search would be your God. The common creeds and declarations describe the shared faith of multitudes, but if you wished to know what you personally believe and act upon, to know what God is to you, your own memory and your own anticipation would have to be consulted rather than public documents. You would ask yourself ultimately about your mental image of God, what God once was for you, what he is to you now, what you expect of him.

John S. Dunne, A Search for God in Time and Memory *(Indiana: Notre Dame Press, 1977) pp.vii-viii*

- A young girl once stood on a beach in Normandy, facing the sea and singing. The poet W.B. Yeats stood behind her at a distance, listening to her song. She sang of the many civilisations that had existed there and passed away, he tells us. She sang to words of her own, but she ended each verse with the cry, "O Lord, let something remain."

- If you were to write your own creed, your own personal "I believe in…", what would be the source of your affirmations?

- Can you think of an experience or event in your personal life, painful at the time it happened, that you are now grateful for as you look back on it?

- Can you think of an experience in your life, which you thought wonderful at the time, but now regret because of the unseen consequences?

- What would you change in your past story if you had the chance? How would you revise your own history? Would that revision change who you are today?

- Given who you are today, how would you write your birth narrative so that it would let people know who you have become?

REFLECTION: LITTLE GIDDING
BY T. S. ELIOT (EXCERPT)

What we call the beginning is often the end
And to make an end is to make a beginning.
The end is where we start from. And every phrase
And sentence that is right
(where every word is at home,
Taking its place to support the others,
The word neither diffident nor ostentatious,
An easy commerce of the old and the new,
The common word exact without vulgarity,
The formal word precise but not pedantic,
The complete consort dancing together)
Every phrase and every sentence is
an end and a beginning,
Every poem an epitaph. And any action
Is a step to the block, to the fire, down the sea's throat
Or to an illegible stone: and that is where we start.
We die with the dying:

See, they depart, and we go with them.
We are born with the dead:
See, they return, and bring us with them.
The moment of the rose and the moment of the yew-tree
Are of equal duration. A people without history
Is not redeemed from time, for history is a pattern
Of timeless moments. So, while the light fails
On a winter's afternoon, in a secluded chapel
History is now and England.

With the drawing of this Love
and the voice of this Calling

We shall not cease from exploration
And the end of all our exploring
Will be to arrive where we started
And know the place for the first time.

H. Gardner (ed.), **The Faber Book of Religious Verse** *(London: Faber & Faber, 1972) p.319*

THE INFANCY NARRATIVES

1) In the early preaching of the Church there is no mention of what preceded Jesus' public ministry, nothing about his birth or hidden life. This absence allows two evangelists, Matthew and Luke, to exercise great freedom in the composition of their infancy narratives as their introduction to the life and significance of Jesus the Christ. The one they *now* believe to be Lord and Messiah is the one whose birth they celebrate.

2) **Similarities between Matthew and Luke**
   a) *Mary is the mother of Jesus; Joseph is considered to be the father* (Mt 1:21, 25; Lk 2:16, 41, 48)
   b) *The conception of the child is through the Holy Spirit* (Mt 1:20-25; Lk 1:26-38)
   c) *The name of the child, Jesus, is given by God through an angel* (Mt 1:21 to Joseph; Lk 1:31 to Mary)
   d) *Jesus belongs to the family of David* (Mt 1:1-17; Lk 1:32)
   e) *The birth takes place in Bethlehem in Judea* (Mt 2:1; Lk 2:4-6)
   f) *The birth is related to the reign of Herod the Great* (Mt 2:1; Lk 1:5)
   g) *The child is reared in Nazareth* (Mt 2:23; Lk 2:39)

3) **Differences between Matthew and Luke**
   a) The genealogy of Matthew (1:1-17), which goes back to Abraham, is quite unlike the genealogy of Luke, which goes back to Adam (3:23-38).
   b) In Matthew, Joseph is the recipient of revelation. In Luke, Mary is the recipient, and Joseph is described as the one who stands by.
   c) According to Matthew, Joseph and Mary originally live in Judea. According to Luke, they live in Nazareth. Matthew has to get the family from Bethlehem to Nazareth, while Luke has to get the family from Nazareth to Bethlehem.
   d) None of the events mentioned in Matthew 2 are mentioned by Luke: the visit of the Magi, an evil Herod, the flight into Egypt, the massacre of the innocents, the return from Egypt, the avoidance of Judea under Archelaus. (Joseph, the legal father, like Joseph the patriarch, dreams and escapes to Egypt. Jesus, like Moses, is delivered from the hands of a wicked king who slaughtered male infants. Jesus, like Moses, is "called out of Egypt". Thus, Jesus is seen to relive the history of his own people.)
   e) Matthew does not celebrate the birth of John the Baptist, which occupies about half of Luke's infancy narrative. Neither does Matthew mention the census, the shepherds, the visitation, the presentation in the Temple, the loss and finding of Jesus in the Temple. Luke's three hymns - the *Benedictus* of Zechariah, the *Magnificat* of Mary, and the *Nunc Dimittis* of Simeon - are not found in Matthew.

4) As history, the two infancy narratives are irreconcilable. As faith-filled celebrations of **who Jesus is**, they are both theological masterpieces. Both narratives convey the good news of salvation, and in that sense they are truly "Gospel". As we saw from the study of early Christology, the earliest preaching celebrated the resurrection as the moment when Jesus was "made Lord" and "designated" as God's Son. As Christian

faith developed and deepened, the moments of Jesus' life (death and resurrection; baptism; conception and birth) became occasions for clarifying the identity of Jesus as anointed king of the House of David and Son of God. While Mark celebrates the identity of Jesus at the **moment of Jesus' baptism**, where he is designated by the heavenly voice as Son of God, the infancy narratives celebrate the same truth **at the moments of Jesus' conception and birth.**

So now the *declaration of Sonship* that was first attached to the resurrection and then to the baptism is now made by the angel at the conception of Jesus. The infancy narratives celebrate a theological truth: Jesus was Son of God not only at his resurrection and baptism but also during the entirety of his life.

6) Both infancy narratives are professions of an Easter faith: Jesus is *Christos Kyrios* and Son

Benedetto Bonfigli:
The Adoration of the Kings and Christ on the Cross

of God. Matthew and Luke choose the conception and birth of Jesus as their Christological moment, as their vehicle to communicate the true identity of Jesus. ***In the light of the death and resurrection of Jesus, the past is now celebrated anew.*** This is caught beautifully in Bonfigli's painting. The light of Jesus' last days illuminates the obscurity of his birth: this is not the birth of an ordinary child, but the birth of the one Christian faith proclaims to be the Messiah and Son of God.

7) Both infancy narratives are deliberately set within the wider context of Old Testament prophecy. Thus Matthew and Luke, through their infancy narratives, succeed in making Jesus' history intelligible against a background of Hebrew prophecy and expectation. In their own different ways, they connect the ***new story of Jesus to the old story of Israel***, so that the readers can see that Jesus comes as an answer to the longings and hopes of Israel.

8) Both evangelists do more than establish a connection with Israel. They also celebrate the truth that emerged only after much discussion and contest in the early Church: ***that Jesus comes not only as the glory of Israel but also as the light to enlighten all peoples.*** The presence of the magi in Matthew's Gospel and the voice of Simeon in Luke's Gospel both tell the readers the significance of Jesus for the whole of humanity. Alongside that, the infancy narratives contain the warning that not everyone will accept the Gospel. In Matthew's narrative the king, the chief priests and the scribes are shown to be hostile to Jesus. In Luke's narrative Simeon warns that the child Jesus is set for the fall as well as the rise of many in Israel. Thus the birth stories contain the summary of the whole Gospel.

FURTHER READING

A. Graffy,   *Trustworthy and True: The Gospels beyond 2000* (Dublin: Columba, 2001) pp.165-185

D. McBride,   "The Infancy Narrative: the Visit of God in Jesus" in *Emmaus* pp. 30-46; *The Gospel of Luke* (Dublin: Dominican Publications, 1997) pp. 20-49

R.E. Brown,   *The Birth of the Messiah,* 2nd Edition (London: Chapman, 1993)

REFLECTION: EPIPHANY
BY R.S. THOMAS

*Three kings? Not even one
any more. Royalty
has gone to ground, its journeyings
over. Who now will bring*

*gifts and to what place? In
the manger there are only the toys
and the tinsel. The child
has become a man. Far*

*off from his cross in the wrong
season he sits at table
with us with on his head
the fool's cap of our paper money.*

R.S. Thomas, Collected Poems 1945–1966 (London: Phoenix, 1966) p.363

Shown on the left is a bronze sculpture of the meeting of the two mothers, made to celebrate the new millennium, which stands outside the Church of the Visitation in Ein Karim, in Israel. The two mothers, Mary and Elizabeth, greet one another with their eyes. As the two women meet with their eyes, their wombs are in closest contact with each other. Elizabeth stands, arms outstretched by her side, a glowing exhibition of a mother-to-be. Mary holds her own womb. This is not just the meeting of two women, but the meeting of two testaments, the Old and the New. The New Testament has come to visit the Old Testament. This is also the meeting between two babes in the womb: John the Baptist, the last of the great prophets, and the greater one he will herald, the one who is Lord.

THE STRUCTURE OF LUKE'S INFANCY NARRATIVE

16

Luke uses the first two chapters of his Gospel to build a bridge between the old story of Israel and the new story of Jesus. Matthew begins his Gospel with Abraham, and Luke does the same, except that he retells the story of Abraham and Sarah through the characters of Zechariah and Elizabeth. With both couples, the situation involves old age, barrenness, and the gift of a child; an angel announces the forthcoming conception to the father; the father asks: "How am I to know this?" (see Gen 15:8); and the final rejoicing of the mother is celebrated. Four Old Testament characters – Zechariah, Elizabeth, Simeon and Anna – cross the bridge from the Old Testament and connect the story of Israel to the new story of Israel.

The Mary/Jesus story is also closely patterned on the Hannah/Samuel story. As Hannah brought Samuel to the central sanctuary to present him to God and he was received by the ancient Eli (1 Sam 1:25; 2:11), so also Mary presents Jesus at the Temple sanctuary to be received by the ancient Simeon. Both Jesus and Samuel are described as becoming full of strength and progressing in favour "before God and man" (1 Sam 2:21, 26; Lk 2:40, 52).

Set amidst Old Testament references, the infancy narrative demonstrates the belief that God acts through his Son, Jesus, in the same way that he has acted in the past. In Jesus these two stories of old and new Israel, these two testaments, are united, for Jesus comes not only as the glory of Israel but a light to enlighten the Gentiles.

This is summarised exquisitely in the story of the visitation. The mother of the new Israel journeys to meet a mother of old Israel, the mother of the last of the great prophets. The two of them are related, as the Old Testament is related to the New Testament. Mary greets Elizabeth and the latter hails Mary: "Of all women you are the most blessed, and blessed is the fruit of your womb" (Lk 1:42). Elizabeth recognises Mary as "mother of my Lord" (Lk 1:43). As the adult John the Baptist will lead others to the one who is greater, so the child in the womb leaps for joy and leads his mother to recognise Jesus as Lord. In their greeting and recognition, the two testaments celebrate one another.

Story of old Israel	Event	Story of new Israel

• Place is Judea, in Temple
• Parents are introduced:
  – Zechariah (a priest)
  – Elizabeth (old and barren)
• The son is introduced
  and named:
  John: great before the Lord
• Sign: Zechariah is silenced
	Birth Annunciations	• Place is Galilee, in Nazareth
		• Parents are introduced:
		  – Joseph (of the house of David)
		  – Mary (a young virgin)
		• The son is introduced
		  and named:
		  Jesus: great; Son of God
		• Sign: old kinswoman is pregnant

• Elizabeth as mother/sign
• Response of blessing:
  "mother of my Lord"
	The Visitation	• Mary travels to Judah
		• Response of Magnificat:
		  "Almighty has done great…"

• Birth of John
• Joy over the birth
  (neighbours and relatives)
	The Birth of the Children	• Birth of Jesus
		• Joy over the birth
		  (angels and shepherds)

• John is circumcised
  and named
• Response of the Benedictus
• Hidden life of John
  the Baptist
• Lives in wilderness until
  appears to Israel
	Circumcision and Naming	• Jesus is circumcised and
		  named

• Temple in Jerusalem • Simeon waits to see • "glory of people Israel" • Simeon prophesies about child • Old Anna speaks about child	**The Presentation in the Temple** **LAW** **SPIRIT**	• Joseph, Mary and Jesus • "Christ the Lord" • "light to enlighten Gentiles" • "sign destined for rejection" • "deliverance of Jerusalem" • Hidden life of Jesus

• Temple - Passover
• Jesus stays in the Temple
• He questions doctors
  of the Law
• Doctors astounded by
  intelligence
	Conflict in the Temple	• The parents and Jesus
		• Parents look among relatives
		• Parents question Jesus
		• Parents don't understand
		• Hidden life of Jesus

17

LUKE'S INFANCY NARRATIVE: THREE NOTES

1) For his two annunciation narratives, Luke adopts the Old Testament literary pattern for stories of annunciation, which can be seen as follows:

- Revelation is marked by the presence of an angel
- Visionary reacts with fear
- Angel counsels visionary: "Do not be afraid…"
- Announcement that woman will give birth to a son
- The name to be given the child
- The future accomplishments of the child
- The visionary makes an objection
- The objection is overruled
- The response/return of the visionary

2) **Sign of "swaddling clothes"**

The swaddling clothes, Luke says, are given as a sign to the shepherds. That sign points back to King Solomon:

"I too, when I was born, drew in the common air. I fell on the same ground that bears us all, a wail my first sound, as for all the rest. I was nurtured in swaddling clothes, with every care. No king has known any other beginning of existence: for all there is one way only into life, as out of it." (Wis 7:3-6)

Solomon's description of birth, focusing on the detail of the swaddling clothes, is important because of who he is: he is a royal child, a son of David. The swaddling clothes, therefore, have the function of a sign because they point not to the poverty of the parents but to the royalty of the child.

3) **Sign of "manger"**

The manger, Luke says, is given as a sign to the shepherds. That sign points back to Isaiah:

"The ox knows its owner and the ass its master's crib; but Israel does not know me, my people does not understand me." (Is 1:3)

In this text the dumb animals are better at recognising their owner than the people of Israel are at recognising the visitation of their Lord. The manger becomes, for Luke, a symbol for the recognition of the Lord by his people. The shepherds stand for the kind of people Jesus will reach out to during his ministry. The fact that the shepherds recognise the manger as a sign of the birth of their saviour is an indication that, unlike the Israel of the past, they do know the manger of their Lord.

FURTHER READING

D. McBride,   *The Gospel of Luke* (Dublin: Dominican Publications, 1997) pp. 20-49

J. Fitzmyer,   *The Gospel according to Luke, 1-9* (New York: Doubleday, 1981) pp. 303ff; "Problems in the Lucan Infancy Narrative" in *Luke the Theologian* (London: Chapman, 1989) pp. 27-50

18 JOHN THE BAPTIST & JESUS IN THE GOSPELS

Ketut Lasia (Bali):
The Baptism of Jesus (detail)

It is one thing to state that John would not be very significant historically if he had not had some contact with Jesus, but it is another thing to accept the Gospel's presentation of John, in which he is a kind of proto-Christian pointing the way to Jesus as Messiah. The Gospel writers wish us to believe that John really had no importance whatsoever in his own right and that his importance was entirely the result of witnessing to the arrival of the Messiah...

Since mention of John the Baptist in the New Testament is obviously overlaid with a developing insistence on Jesus' superiority, we can suppose that the issue of John himself was a problem for the early Church. Clearly John was not a nobody in his time, and the Gospels accord him respect. However, John was not permitted too much respect; people had to know his place. Most often the interpretations aim at neutralizing the Baptist's independence to make him safe for Christianity.

(J. Taylor, *John the Baptist within the Second Temple Period* (London: SPCK, 1997) pp.2,5)

John's place in the three stages of Gospel formation

In all four Gospels John the Baptist is presented as a key *transitional* figure in the story of the adult Jesus, standing between the hidden life of Jesus and his public ministry. Because John is such a significant character at the beginning of Jesus' public life, he stands as a turning point in the three stages of the Gospel tradition:

Stage 1   The public ministry of Jesus
John the Baptist **(JB)** >
death and resurrection

Stage 2   The apostolic preachers
Death and resurrection >
John the Baptist **(JB)**

Stage 3   The evangelists
- *Mark:*
  JB > death and resurrection
- *Matthew:* Infancy
  JB > death and resurrection
- *Luke:* Infancy (beginning with JB)
  JB > death and resurrection
- *John:* Prologue: Word and Witness
  JB > death and resurrection

Two key texts, both in the form of speeches by Peter, situate the unique place of John the Baptist in the Christian story:

Acts 1:21-22:

*"We must therefore choose someone who has been with us the whole time the Lord Jesus was travelling around with us, someone who was with us **right from the time when John was baptising** until the day when he was taken up from us – and he can act as a witness to the resurrection."*

Acts 10:36-37:

*"You must have heard about the recent happening in Judea, about Jesus of Nazareth and how he **began in Galilee, after John had been preaching baptism.**"*

The context of Jesus' beginning

It is interesting to recall how Jesus of Nazareth began. To understand the beginning of the story of the adult Jesus, the four Gospels point us to someone else, the figure of John the Baptist. John the Baptist is the independent prophetic force that stands between the hidden life of Jesus and his public ministry. Jesus does not begin alone; none of us does. Jesus, like many other people, is attracted by the person and preaching of John the Baptist; like many of his contemporaries, he submits to John's baptism of repentance for the forgiveness of sins. After his association with John, Jesus' life takes a dramatic turn. He follows John in the prophetic vocation and reinterprets the message of his mentor.

Versus		
• the city of Jerusalem		• the wilderness
• the Temple (ritual sacrifice)		• River Jordan (ritual: baptism)
• the priestly		• the prophetic (focus: word of God)
• the institutional		• the charismatic
• the temporal power		• the religious critic
• the aristocracy		• the marginalised
• the settled		• the nomadic

The four Gospels have their own way of limiting the embarrassing memory of Jesus becoming a convert of the Baptist. By the time the Gospels are written John is domesticated within the Christian story and his role is defined simply as a forerunner of Jesus. But John's independent ministry among the people, the moral authority he exercised and the respect he commanded, all still linger in the Gospel tradition. John's place is assured at the beginning of the Gospel as the nomadic prophet who attracted Jesus from his settled life in Nazareth. Jesus' beginning was not a solitary event in a landscape empty of people. Like many others, Jesus was attracted by John's reputation and was moved to journey to see this fiery reformer who spoke the word of God with authority.

And after he saw John, Jesus' life was to take a new direction.
A picture emerges of John as a charismatic leader whose great popularity among the people is exercised apart from Jesus. His ministry begins before Jesus, and when John dies he leaves behind him a religious following that exists independently of Christianity.

John's ministry dominates the beginning of the Gospel, and the fact that Jesus submits to John's baptism clearly indicates that Jesus accepted the Baptist's message calling Israel to repentance. As an independent prophet, John displays no discernible respect for religious hierarchy and he appears alienated from institutional religion. His natural sanctuary is the wilderness, not the Temple; his ritual act centres around the waters of the river, not around the priestly altar of sacrifice. John's alienation from normal society is underscored by his ascetic lifestyle in an uninhabited place, his Bedouin dress of animal skin and his peasant diet of locusts and wild honey. The composite picture of John and his ministry that emerges from the Gospels seems to set a stage of conflict, one that Jesus will enter on the side of John.

This stage of conflict is already established before Jesus begins his ministry. When Jesus walks on to the stage, he chooses to stand beside the wild man of the wilderness, an option that will soon alienate him from institutional religion. That is why it is worth recalling what all the Gospels note: *Jesus begins after John.*

THE GOSPEL OF MARK
(about AD 70)

1)   Opens the Gospel about Jesus with the story of John the Baptist. (See Acts 1:21 and 10:37 where the beginning of Jesus' story means the time of JB's ministry.)

2)   1:4   Wilderness: JB proclaims a baptism of repentance for forgiveness of sins.

3)   1:5   All Judea and all people of Jerusalem go to JB They are baptised by him and they confess their sins to him. (JB is shown as major religious authority.)

4)   1:6   JB's wardrobe (see 2 Kings 1:8) and diet.

5)   1:7   In the course of JB's preaching: "Someone is following me, someone who is greater…"

6)   1:8   "I baptise with water, he will baptise with the Holy Spirit."

7)   1:9   Jesus comes from Nazareth and is baptised by JB
         a) divine proclamation
         b) Spirit descends
         c) Jesus is declared God's son
         (Ps. 2:7 "He said to me, 'You are my son, today I have begotten you'")

8)   1:14   Jesus stays south until JB is arrested. He then goes to Galilee and starts preaching: "The kingdom of God is close… repent and believe…"

9)   2:18   JB's disciples and Pharisees fast: Jesus' disciples do not.

10)   6:16   Some people, including Herod, think that Jesus is JB risen.

11)   6:17   JB is arrested and he is beheaded at the request of Herodias.

12)   6:29   The disciples of John lay his body in the tomb.

13)   9:13   "Elijah has come, and they have treated him as they pleased…"

14)   11:31   Questioned about his authority, Jesus speaks of John's baptism.

THE GOSPEL OF MATTHEW
(about AD 80)

1)   Opens Gospel with genealogy of Jesus, which he takes back to Abraham. Matthew then develops his infancy narrative by establishing **who Jesus is** (chapter 1) and **where he is from** (chapter 2). JB is not mentioned.

2)   3:1   JB appears in the wilderness of Judea.
         His message: "Repent, for the kingdom of heaven is close at hand."

3)   3:4   JB's wardrobe (see 2 Kings 2:1-18) and diet. (In the tradition of Elijah.)

4)   3:5   Jerusalem, Judea and Jordan district make way to JB. They are baptised by him and confess their sins to him.

5)   3:7   Rebukes religious leaders: fruits, not roots.

6)   3:11   "I baptise with water… but the one who follows me is more powerful… he will baptise with the Holy Spirit and fire."

7)   3:13   Jesus comes from Galilee for baptism. JB objects, but Jesus gives permission.
         a) heavens are opened
         b) Spirit descends
         c) voice speaks: "This is my son…"

	4:12	*When JB is arrested, Jesus returns to Galilee.*
		His message: **"Repent, for the kingdom of God is close at hand."**
9)	9:14	*Jesus is questioned by JB's disciples about fasting etc.*
10)	11:2	*JB's question to Jesus: "Are you the one who is to come?" Jesus on JB: "Of all children, greater than JB never seen... He is Elijah who was to return".*
11)	11:16	*Differences between JB and Son of Man.*
12)	14:1	*Herod speaks of Jesus to his court: "This is JB himself..."*
		JB is beheaded at request of Herodias, and Jesus withdraws to a lonely place.
12)	16:14	*Crowds say Jesus is JB*
13)	17:13	*The disciples understand Jesus to mean that JB is Elijah.*
14)	21:32	*Jesus criticises the chief priests and elders for not believing in John.*

THE GOSPEL OF LUKE
(about AD 85)

1)	1&2	Infancy narrative: opens story of child Jesus with the story of child JB
		Diptych of annunciation, birth, circumcision, naming.
		Identity: JB is great before the Lord; Jesus is Great, Christ the Lord, Son of God.
2)	3:1	Opens story of adult Jesus with story of adult JB in wilderness.
3)	3:3	JB goes through the Jordan valley, preaching a baptism of repentance.
4)	3:7	Message to crowd: "Produce fruit; axe is laid to the roots of the trees."
5)	3:10	All the people ask JB: "What must we do then?"
6)	3:15	People's expectancy: JB is the Christ (see Acts 13:25) JB: "Someone..."
7)	3:19	JB criticises Herod for many crimes. He is imprisoned.
8)	3:21	After people are baptised and after Jesus is baptised, he is at prayer.
		a) heavens open
		b) Spirit descends
		c) voice speaks: "You are my son..."
9)	3:38	Ancestry of Jesus is taken back to first human, "son of Adam, son of God".
10)	5:33	"JB's disciples are always fasting and praying, but yours go on eating..."
11)	7:18	JB sends disciples from prison with question: "Are you the one?"
12)	7:28	Jesus says of JB: "Of all children born of woman, no one is greater than John; yet least in the kingdom of God is greater than he is."
13)	7:33	Differences between JB and Son of Man.
14)	9:7	Some people are saying Jesus is JB risen from the dead.
15)	9:19	To question, "Who do crowd say I am?", first answer is JB.
16)	11:1	"Lord, teach us to pray, just as John taught his disciples."
17)	16:16	Up to JB was Law and Prophets, since then the kingdom of God.
18)	20:1	Questioned about his authority, Jesus speaks about JB's baptism.

THE GOSPEL OF JOHN
(about AD 100)

1)   *Opens Gospel not with the genealogy of Jesus, but with the proclamation that the* **Word** *is the creator and ancestor of all humankind.*
Identity of Jesus: Word was God.
Function of Word: Creator and ancestor of all.

2)   1:6   **John's identity:** *man sent by God.* **His function:** *a witness.*
He is not the light, only a witness to speak for the light.
(This Gospel never calls him **the Baptist;** *his function is to witness to Jesus.)*

3)   1:15   *As witness, John proclaims: "This is the One…"*

4)   1:20   *John declares: "I am* **not** *the Christ;* **not** *the prophet;* **not** *Elijah."*

5)   1:26   *Jesus is unknown figure in a crowd of John's followers.*
"There stands among you - unknown to you - the one who follows me."

6)   1:29   *John identifies Jesus, admitting he did not know him by himself.*

7)   1:34   *John: "I am the witness that he is the Chosen One of God."*

8)   1:35   **The first disciples of Jesus are ex-disciples of John.**

9)   3.22   *John and Jesus participate in same ministry of baptism.*
Jesus baptises in Judea. John baptises in Samaria.

10)   3:26   **"The man with you** *on the far side of the Jordan* **is baptising now."**
John's testimony as a witness 3:28-36.

11)   4:2   *A redactor denies that Jesus was baptising.*

12)   4:38   *Jesus' disciples reap harvest in Samaria they have not laboured for.*

13)   5:31   *Jesus compares his testimony to that of John as his witness.*

14)   10:40   *To escape arrest, Jesus returns to John's old place on far side of Jordan.*
Many testify to John's effective witness and believe in Jesus.

Caravaggio painted a series of pictures of solitary saints. His painting on the left, Saint John the Baptist, *was completed towards the end of his Roman career and during his exile, probably about 1603. The seated figure of John is set among cavernous shadows that encroach on him and mask his eyes. He is dressed in animal skin, and lush red drapery falls in long vertical folds around him. This is the solitary, brooding John, whose stillness challenges us to wonder about his wondering.*

By contrast, Andrea del Sarto's earlier painting of John the Baptist (1528), on the right, shows the youthful John emerging from the dark rock face, dressed in animal skin. He stands attentive and ready for action, his eyes fixed beyond himself, in expectation. His water bowl is ready in his right hand.

Special note on Jesus and John in the Fourth Gospel

Eusebius (AD 263-340), bishop of Caesarea, was a Greek Christian writer, born in Palestine and educated in Caesarea. In his *History of the Church* he has a section on the Gospels, and an intriguing theory about why John wrote his Gospel:

"And when Mark and Luke had now published their gospels, John, we are told, who hitherto had relied entirely on the spoken word, finally took to writing for the following reason. The three gospels already written were in general circulation and copies had come into John' hands. He welcomed them, we are told, and confirmed their accuracy, but remarked that the narrative only lacked the story of what Christ had done first of all at the beginning of His mission.

"This tradition is undoubtedly true. Anyone can see that the three evangelists have recorded the doings of the Saviour for only one year, following the consignment of John the Baptist to prison, and that they indicated this very fact at the beginning of their narrative...

"We are told, then, that for this reason the apostle John was urged to record in his gospel the period which the earlier evangelists had passed over in silence and the things done during that period by the Saviour, i.e. all that happened before the Baptist's imprisonment; that this is indicated first by his words: 'Thus did Jesus begin His miracles', and later by mentioning the Baptist, in the middle of his account of Jesus' doings, as then still baptising at Aenon near Salim; and that he makes this plainer when he adds 'for John had not yet been thrown into gaol'.

"Thus *John in his gospel narrative records what Christ did when the Baptist had not yet been thrown into gaol, while the other three evangelists describe what happened after the Baptist's consignment to prison.* Once this is grasped, there no longer appears to be a discrepancy between the gospels, because John's deals with the early stages of Christ's career and the others cover the last period of His story."
(*The History of the Church 3, 24*)

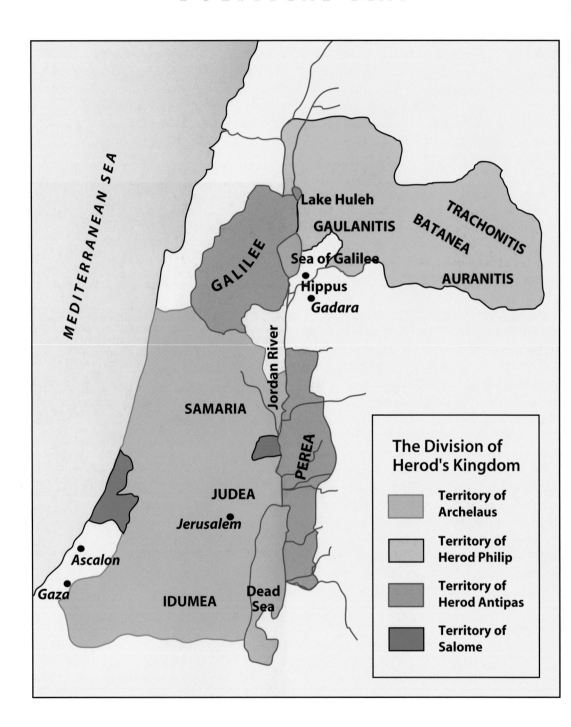

The map shows:

- MEDITERRANEAN SEA
- Lake Huleh
- GALILEE
- GAULANITIS
- TRACHONITIS
- BATANEA
- Sea of Galilee
- AURANITIS
- Hippus
- Gadara
- Jordan River
- SAMARIA
- PEREA
- JUDEA
- Jerusalem
- Ascalon
- Gaza
- IDUMEA
- Dead Sea

The Division of Herod's Kingdom

- Territory of Archelaus
- Territory of Herod Philip
- Territory of Herod Antipas
- Territory of Salome

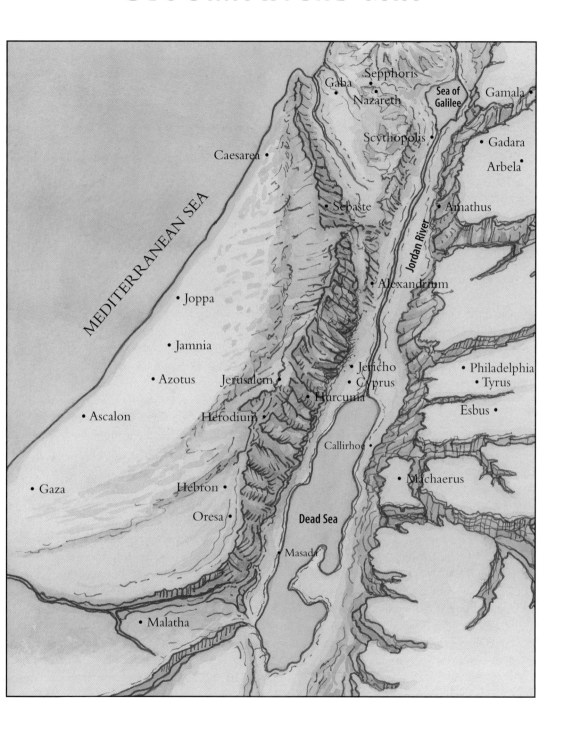

Gaba
Sepphoris
Nazareth
Sea of Galilee
Gamala
Scythopolis
Gadara
Arbela
Caesarea
Sebaste
Amathus
MEDITERRANEAN SEA
Jordan River
Alexandrium
Joppa
Jamnia
Jericho
Philadelphia
Cyprus
Tyrus
Azotus
Jerusalem
Hurcumia
Esbus
Ascalon
Herodium
Callirhoe
Gaza
Machaerus
Hebron
Oresa
Dead Sea
Masada
Malatha

THE BAPTISM OF JESUS

1) Through both the simple and the wonderful elements (see diagram) the evangelists combine experience of Jesus being baptised and the significance they accord that event. Thus experience and meaning, event and significance, are combined in one story. The wonderful element interprets for the readers the significance of the baptism of Jesus.

2) **Background texts to the baptism**

Psalm 2:7

I will declare the decree of the Lord: He said to me, you are my son, today I have begotten you.

Isaiah 42:1

Behold, my servant whom I have chosen, my beloved with whom my soul is well pleased. I will put my spirit upon him, and he shall proclaim justice to the Gentiles. *(See Matt 12:18.)*

Isaiah 61:1

The Spirit of the Lord has been given to me, for Yahweh has anointed me. He has sent me to bring good news to the poor, to bind up hearts that are broken.

Isaiah 63:7–64:12

The Prayer of Israel: Where is he who brought out of the sea the shepherd of his flock? Where is he who endowed him with his Holy Spirit?… Look down from heaven, look down, for you are our Father…

Our Redeemer is your ancient name. Do not let your compassion go unmoved, for you are our Father… O that you would tear the heavens open and come down… To make known your name… Zion is wilderness… Can you go unmoved by all this, oppressing us by your silence?

3) At every baptism, we believe as Christians in something that we do not actually see, in something that cannot be recorded by the senses. We believe that:

- **The heavens do open**
- **The Spirit does descend**
- **The voice of God does recognise the baptised as son/daughter**

The wonderful elements that are shown to be part of the baptism of Jesus form part of our belief in *what is going on* during the sacrament. But *what is going on* cannot be seen in *what is actually taking place;* the significance of the moment is not evident from observing the event. No outsider, observing the action of the sacrament, could guess at the divine action it heralds.

The Synoptic accounts bring out the significance of the baptism of Jesus by *showing* it, by painting it in vivid colours like an artist. But there is never a suggestion in those same accounts that anyone else observes this; neither do other people ever say during the public ministry that they know the identity of Jesus because they witnessed or heard about what happened in his baptism. The baptism of Jesus stands as a revelatory story for the *readers* of the Gospel, not the original participants in the story.

At **Stage 1** of the tradition (the public ministry of Jesus) John the Baptist baptises Jesus, clearly an event that proves to be an embarrassing memory for the later Church.

That memory is recast in **Stage 3** (the writing of the Gospels) not as a baptism by John, but as a baptism by the Spirit – in other words a *Christian* baptism. As Paul wrote before the Gospels were written: "The proof that you are sons is that God has sent the Spirit of his son into our hearts: the Spirit that cries 'Abba Father' and it is this that makes you a son" (Gal 4:6).

Nicolas Poussin (1594-1665) was commissioned by his patron, M de Chantelou, to paint a series of the seven sacraments. The above painting, Sacrament of Baptism, *is in the National Gallery of Scotland, Edinburgh, together with the remaining six. At the centre of the painting you can see Jesus submitting to the baptism of John (Stage 1) while those immediately around them look on at the event. The further out you go from the centre, you notice that the people are looking not at John baptising Jesus, but the Spirit descending on him from above (Stage 3). The artist Poussin can be seen behind the kneeling Jesus, watching the event closely.*

simple element		wonderful element
• Jesus leaves home in Galilee and travels south to see John the Baptist		• heavens open
• With many others, he is baptised by John in the river Jordan		• Spirit descends
		• voice declares his identity

JOHN'S INFLUENCE ON JESUS

20

1) How Jesus followed John the Baptist: Like John, Jesus:

- remained unmarried and followed a calling in prophetic tradition
- preached out of doors
- remained independent of other religious groups
- preached: "Repent, for the kingdom of heaven is close at hand"
- gathered his own disciples
- baptised with water
- confronted religious authorities
- opened up new life for tax collectors, prostitutes, etc.
- questioned special place of Israel, rejecting nationalism
- was rejected by Pharisees and leaders
- rejected the self-righteous and accepted notorious sinners
- gave disciples prayer to characterise them
- was believed to be the Messiah
- was handed over and executed by civil powers
- was believed to be risen from the dead

2) How Jesus differed from John the Baptist

- John was ascetic, associated with the wilderness
- John proclaimed judgement
- John belonged to realm of law
- John remained in expectation time
- John was not associated with healing or exorcism

- Jesus ate and drank with sinners in towns and villages
- Jesus proclaimed love and mercy
- Jesus began the Gospel
- Jesus brought fulfilment time
- Jesus healed and exorcised: "If by the finger of God I cast out devils, the kingdom of God is among you" (Lk 11:20).

3) Two different perceptions, reflecting two different times?

The people in the pages of the Gospel witness to the similarities between Jesus and John. The most popular guess about Jesus' real identity by the ordinary people and by Herod Antipas is that Jesus is John the Baptist. The presumption is expressed that Jesus will follow John also in his ascetic

---

How John the Baptist stands at the turning point of Jesus' life can be seen in the following way:

Jesus before John		Jesus after John
• "This is Joseph's son"	← identity →	• prophet/teacher
• woodworker in hill village of Nazareth	← direction →	• wandering mission to lost sheep of the house of Israel
• loyalty to Judaism and to family	← outlook →	• kingdom of God and new family

lifestyle. The time comes, however, when the differences become so marked that John asks the question: "Are you the one who is to come, or do we have to wait for someone else?" John's question could be a positive development. Only if John previously accepted Jesus as Messiah is his question a negative one. If John did not know Jesus as Messiah, then his question from prison is a positive one: it is wonder at the door of faith.

4) **The death of John the Baptist**

Flavius Josephus, the Jewish historian, was governor of Galilee at the outbreak of the Jewish War in AD 66. In Book 18 of his *Antiquities*, he speaks about John the Baptist in a passage that is twice as long as the earlier one on Jesus. He makes no connection between the two men. He explains that Herod Antipas executed John because the tetrarch was afraid of the Baptist's enormous popularity among the people:

"For Herod killed him, although he was a good man and bade the Jews to join in baptism, providing that they were cultivating virtue and practising justice towards one another and piety towards God . . . And when ordinary Jews gathered around John - for their excitement reached fever pitch as they listened to his words - Herod began to fear that John's powerful ability to persuade people might lead to some sort of revolt, for they seemed likely to do whatever he counselled. So Herod decided to do away with John first, before he sparked a revolt. Herod considered this a better course of action than to wait until the situation changed and then to regret his delay. And so, because of Herod's suspicion, John was sent in chains to Machaerus, the mountain fortress previously mentioned; there he was killed."

(Flavius Josephus, Antiquities, *18.5.2*)

READING

C. Evans,	"Context, family and formation" in *The Cambridge Companion to Jesus* (Cambridge: Cambridge University Press, 2001)
J. Taylor,	*John the Baptist within the Second Temple Period* (London: SPCK, 1997)
W.B. Tatum,	*John the Baptist and Jesus* (Sonoma: Poleridge Press, 1994)
J.P. Meier,	"John without Jesus" and "Jesus with and without John" in *A Marginal Jew: Rethinking the Historical Jesus,* Vol. 2 (New York: Doubleday, 1994) pp. 19-177
J.D. Crossan,	"John and Jesus" in *The Historical Jesus* (Edinburgh: T&T Clark, 1991) pp. 227-264
J. Murphy-O'Connor,	"John the Baptist and Jesus: History and Hypotheses" in *New Testament Studies* 36 (1990) pp. 359-374
E. Schillebeeckx,	*Jesus* (London: Collins, 1979) pp. 126-139
R.E. Brown,	"John the Baptist in the Gospel of John" in *New Testament Essays* (New York: Doubleday, 1968) pp. 174-184
J. Fitzmyer,	"The Lucan Picture of John the Baptist" in *Luke the Theologian* pp. 86-110

REFLECTION: LEAVING, LOSS, HOME

When we think of loss we think of the loss, through death, of people we love. But loss is a far more encompassing theme in our life. For we lose not only through death, but also by leaving and being left, by changing and letting go and moving on. And our losses include not only our separations and departures from those we love, but our conscious and unconscious losses of romantic dreams, impossible expectations, illusions of freedom and power, illusions of safety – and the loss of our own younger self, the self that thought it always would be unwrinkled and invulnerable and immortal.

These losses we confront when we are confronted by the inescapable fact...

that our mother is going to leave us, and we will leave her;

that our mother's love can never be ours alone; that what hurts us cannot always be kissed and made better;

that we are essentially out here on our own; that we will have to accept – in other people and ourselves – the mingling of love with hate, of the good with the bad;

that no matter how wise and beautiful and charming a girl may be, she still cannot grow up to marry her dad;

that our options are constricted by anatomy and guilt;

that there are flaws in every human connection; that our status on this planet is implacably impermanent;

and that we are utterly powerless to offer ourselves or those we love protection – protection from danger and pain, from the in-roads of time, from the coming of age, from the coming of death; protection from our necessary losses.

These losses are a part of life – universal, unavoidable, inexorable. And these losses are necessary because we grow by losing and leaving and letting go.

For the road to human development is paved with renunciation. Throughout our life we grow by giving up. We give up some of our deepest attachments to others. We give up certain cherished parts of ourselves. We must confront, in the dreams we dream, as well as in our intimate relationships, all that we never will have and never will be. Passionate investment leaves us vulnerable to loss. And sometimes, no matter how clever we are, we must lose.

J. Viorst, **Necessary Losses** *(New York: Simon & Schuster, 1986) pp.15-16*

REFLECTION: HOME IS SO SAD
BY PHILIP LARKIN

Home is so sad. It stays as it was left,
Shaped to the comfort of the last to go
As if to win them back. Instead, bereft
Of anyone to please, it withers so,
Having no heart to put aside the theft

And turn again to what it started as,
A joyous shot at how things ought to be,
Long fallen wide. You can see how it was:
Look at the pictures and the cutlery.
The music in the piano stool. That vase.

Philip Larkin, The Whitsun Weddings *(London: Faber & Faber, 1979) p.17*

REFLECTION: ON LEAVING
REFLECTIONS OF A YOUNG PRIEST

"When I look back at the beginning of my vocation, when I left for seminary, I am surprised at the way my attitudes changed to my family and the world they lived in.

"After all, I was going, leaving, heading off for this new adventure of saving the world. I was engaged by this energetic endeavour, this messianic cause, anxious to make my mark on the world.

"You turn and look at them, your family, and with all the arrogance of the new convert, you suddenly see their lives as little, sort of unimportant beside your vital enterprise. You now see them as people caught, trapped in the endless round of ordinary time. They look unfree; but you are relieved that they cannot keep you or hold you. They look at you, without anger or resentment, perhaps pleased that you are breaking out, or wondering secretly what madness has caught hold of you. You leave for the great outdoors, leaving them behind you in their tiny living room of a world.

"You meet new people, travel to different places, and learn new languages. You become educated in the art of philosophy and the history of religion and the science of theology. You struggle with the great questions that have burdened humankind since the beginning.

"And when you go home you find that their concerns are different: they are worried that the bus-route has changed, that the price of fish has soared, that Uncle John has lost all his teeth and is beginning to go daft in his old age. Their concerns are not yours; your concerns are not theirs. You realise that you and your family live in parallel worlds, with little communication between them.

"Then one day you sit down and read the Gospel story anew. You find it strange that Jesus does not leave his local world for insight. His images are those of every day – a farmer sowing in the field, a woman kneading dough in the kitchen, a son leaving home, a man being mugged on a country road. In reading the Gospels you suspect that you missed something: that it is in the middle of the ordinary that our salvation is being worked; there is nowhere else to work out the purposes of God."

A young priest who wrote to the author, reflecting about his vocation (used with permission)

THE TEMPTATIONS OF JESUS

21

1) The story of the temptations is told in three Gospels as a dramatic preface to the public ministry. The story is set in the wilderness of Judea; apart from Jesus, there are no human actors. In Mark's account there is the simple statement: "The Spirit immediately drove him out into the wilderness. And he was in the wilderness forty days, tempted by Satan; and he was with the wild beasts; and the angels ministered to him" (1:12-13). These two verses are developed in Matthew and Luke, and the story is now told through **three temptations.** John has no story of temptation. Since Matthew's account is considered more original than Luke's, we will concentrate on his telling (4:1-11).

2) In each of the three stories Jesus does not speak his own words but replies with quotations from Deuteronomy, in reverse order.

Jesus' reply to the:
- 1st temptation is Deuteronomy 8:3
- 2nd temptation is Deuteronomy 6:16
- 3rd temptation is Deuteronomy 6:13

As we are signalled back to Deuteronomy we are being told that Deuteronomy holds the key to understanding the story. The context of the temptations is Deuteronomy 8:2-5:

"And you shall remember all the way in which the Lord your God has led you these forty years in the wilderness, that he might humble you, testing you to know what was in your heart, whether you would keep his commandments, or not. And he humbled you and let you hunger and fed you with manna, which you did not know, nor did your fathers know; that he might make you know that man does not live by bread alone, but by everything that proceeds from the mouth of the Lord. Your clothing did not wear out upon you, and your foot did not swell, these forty years. Know then in your heart, that as a man disciplines his son, the Lord your God disciplines you."

The temptations of Jesus are the repetition of the temptation of the chosen people in the wilderness. The Messiah must undergo that ancient testing and bring the history of his people to consummation.

3) **The first temptation**
The first temptation is: "If you are the Son of God, command these stones to become loaves of bread." The key to the meaning of the first story is the idea of hunger, not Jesus' power to work a miracle. It was hunger that was the occasion of the major temptation in the Exodus. The people had experienced a new freedom, but they longed for the food of bondage. Their heart was divided. And this was the question of Jesus. Can you be whole-hearted in following God even when you are hungry? Can you be hungry and still trust? The undividedness of the heart is a priority that Jesus himself will announce: "Set your heart first on the kingdom of God."

4) **The second temptation**
In the second temptation Jesus is challenged to throw himself down from the pinnacle of the Temple. He is asked to endanger his life. The question of *self-preservation* is at the heart of the second temptation. Can you love the love that

loves you even when your life is slipping away? Loving God is not an exemption from harm; it means valuing love more than life and death. In the second temptation the devil suggests that it is possible to serve God while avoiding pain: jump from a great height and land unhurt. Will Jesus be able to avoid suffering and pain and still be faithful to his mission? That is the heart of the second temptation.

5) The third temptation

In the third temptation the devil offers Jesus the kingdoms of the world if Jesus will worship him. Jesus has just opted for an invisible love. He has stated that he will love God even when the sign of love is missing (the bread) and even when he is not protected from diminishment and death. This appears to be a groundless love: what do you have as a sign that you are loved if you have no bread and no guarantee that you will be saved at the last moment?

The devil offers something concrete, tangible: *immediate power*. He tests Jesus about his attitude to power and wealth. But Jesus prefers living in the love he cannot control, rather than accepting the tangible substitutes of power and prestige. Jesus will love the God who loves him even when there is no bread, no protection, and no worldly power.

6) Three temptations, three commands
- The first temptation: **the divided heart**
- The second temptation: **self-preservation**
- The third temptation: **power and wealth**

This triad is enshrined in the great *Shema Israel*, "Hear, O Israel", in Deuteronomy 6:4-5:

> *"Hear, O Israel: the Lord our God is one Lord; and you shall love the Lord your God with all your heart and with all your soul, and with all your might."*

We know how that creed was understood at the time of Jesus because it is quoted and interpreted in the *Mishnah*, an early collection of Jewish teaching material.

With your whole heart:
by this is meant your two inclinations: the good inclination and the dark inclination.

With your whole soul:
by this is meant even if God takes your soul, that is, your life.

With your whole might:
by this is meant your whole property, with all the resources that you have available.

7) Temptation and the ministry of Jesus
These three temptations are a summary of the kind of test that Jesus has to undergo during his ministry, just as his disciples will after him.

Is your heart divided?		
loyalty to family	versus	loyalty to mission
"First let me bury my father"	versus	"Come, follow me"
"Preferring mother and father"	versus	for the sake of the kingdom
Are you prepared to risk your life for the mission?		
Self-preservation and escape	versus	suffering and death
Painless Messiah	versus	"Son of Man must suffer"
Will you worship power and wealth?		
Offer of kingship in Galilee	versus	escaping from power
Mammon (your own treasure)	versus	treasure of the kingdom

8) The origin of the story

We see that Jesus lived through these experiences and was tested in each of these areas: complete dedication, risking his life, living by the values of the kingdom. Who told the story of Jesus' three temptations in the wilderness? Was it Jesus or one of the members of the early Church? The probability is that it was one of the members of the early Church, because Mark simply has Jesus for forty days in the desert, being tempted by Satan. It is hard to believe that if Mark knew the three stories he would have omitted them. But we can visualise, behind the developed stories of Matthew and Luke, Jesus telling his disciples that he was tested as they were going to be tested.

We can imagine Jesus saying, in effect: "I have to struggle with my mission; and commitment for you is going to bring the same trials as it did for me. You are going to be pulled in different ways:

i) *Loyalty to country and family is going to conflict with your loyalty to your vocation.*

ii) *Your desire to save your skin is going to be in tension with what your mission is asking of you.*

iii) *The promise of power and wealth is going to confuse you in your vocation."*

If Jesus had not shared with his disciples his experience of being tested, would his followers have dared to suggest that the Messiah was tempted? It is unlikely that they would move **from the idea of the Messiah** to **the claim the Messiah was tempted**. It is only possible to go from the experience of Jesus to the truth the Messiah was tempted. Only if Jesus had shared his own experience would his followers have believed that the Messiah was tempted.

> *"Therefore he had to be made like his brethren in every respect, so that he might become a merciful and faithful high priest in the service of God, to make expiation for the sins of the people. For because he himself has suffered and been tempted, he is able to help those who are tempted."* (Heb 2:17-18)

The Wilderness of Judea

FURTHER READING

S. Garret,	*The Temptations of Jesus in Mark's Gospel* (Michigan: Eerdmans, 1998)
J. Gibson,	*The Temptations of Jesus in Early Christianity* (Sheffield: Sheffield Academic Press, 1995)
F. Wright Beare,	*The Gospel according to Matthew* (Oxford: Blackwell, 1981) pp. 104-113
J. Fitzmyer,	*The Gospel according to Luke, 1-9*, pp. 506-518
A.B. Taylor,	"Decision in the Desert: The Temptations of Jesus in the light of Deuteronomy" in *Interpretation* 14 (1960) pp. 300-309
D. McBride,	Reflections on the Temptations in *Seasons of the Word* pp. 70-75

THE KINGDOM OF GOD

1) The tradition: earthly or heavenly?

The Synoptic Gospels show Jesus taking up the proclamation of the kingdom of God as soon as John the Baptist is arrested. Where John finishes, Jesus begins: "The kingdom of God is at hand" (Mk 1:15). Most scholars prefer the words "reign" or "sovereignty" as a more precise translation of *basileia* than "kingdom". The word kingdom suggests a territory or a sphere of dominion; reign suggests the active ruling of God in the world. John and Jesus never define what they mean by the kingdom, which suggests the idea was already familiar to their hearers. Certainly, the Jewish people were yearning for the kingdom and expecting it daily. We can distinguish two different but related concepts.

2) An earthly kingdom

This understanding referred back to the promise God made to King David: that after he was gone, God would raise up a son of David, an anointed king, whose throne would be eternal and whose kingdom would be for ever.

"When your days are fulfilled and you lie down with your fathers, I will raise up your son after you, who will come forth from your body and I will establish his kingdom. He shall build a house for my name, and I will establish the throne of his kingdom forever." (2 Sam 7:12-13)

The earliest interpretation understood this kingdom to be earthly, political and exclusive – a military empire of the Jews. But this expectation for a messianic kingdom never materialised; it almost disappeared under the weight of disappointment until the Maccabean revolt (164 BC), which rekindled the old hopes for a political empire. At the time of Jesus, this revived hope, together with the earlier hope that had replaced it, fought for the minds of the Jewish people.

3) A heavenly kingdom

The understanding was expressed in the apocalyptic literature, which flourished during the intertestamental period. This was not an earthly kingdom to be headed by a mortal descendant of David, but a heavenly kingdom to be headed by a celestial figure, one like a son of man.

"I gazed into the visions of the night. And I saw, coming on the clouds of heaven, one like a son of man. He came to the one of great age and was led into his presence. On him was conferred sovereignty, glory and kingship, and men of all peoples, nations and languages became his servants. His sovereignty is an eternal sovereignty which shall never pass away, nor will his empire ever be destroyed." (Dan 7:13-14)

No longer a political, national empire of living Jews, this is a supernatural kingdom which will open its membership to all through a miracle of the resurrection, after a time of agony and trouble (Dan 12:1-2). Preserved from the catastrophe will be a remnant of Israel, the *anawim*, the lowly ones who put their trust in God alone. These are the praying, waiting remnant of Israel. (Luke introduces us to representative figures of the *anawim* in the venerable ancients who people his infancy narrative.)

These are two hopes, two kingdoms. Which one, or which combinations, did the disciples and the people expect when Jesus preached that the kingdom of God was at hand?

4) The kingdom: now or not yet?

In the Gospels it would seem that the people and the disciples looked for the restoration of an earthly kingdom, ruled by the Christ in the tradition of the Davidic dynasty: *"Our own hope had been that he would be the one to set Israel free"* (Lk 24:21). Christ is the title others insist on giving to Jesus, an unqualified title that Jesus does not openly embrace (Mk 8:30). By dramatic contrast Jesus identifies himself openly with the apocalyptic figure of the Son of Man (Mk 2:10, 28; 8:38; 9:9, 12, 31 etc.), as if to reject the earthbound overtones the messianic title contains.

In the person of Jesus, in his deeds and words, the kingdom of God is so near that it is at hand. There are texts that signify not just an approach, but also a real coming into contact:

"If it is by the finger of God that I cast out devils, then the kingdom of God has come upon you." (Lk 11:20; see 10:9)

Jesus is seen to teach that the days of his own ministry are the days of preaching the kingdom of God (Lk 16:16), and that this kingdom will come with power within the lifetime of those listening (Mk 13:32).

If the question of "When?" is difficult to answer, the question of "How?" is somewhat easier. We do not build the kingdom; it is a gift of God. It comes

Byzantine Christ: *The Pantakrator*

neither through personal moral effort nor national political enterprise; it comes from a God of graciousness longing for a response. And that graciousness, the surprise of mercy, is especially addressed to the poor.

5) The kingdom and the poor

"Blessed are you poor for yours is the kingdom of God" (Lk 6:20). In Luke's Gospel the kingdom belongs especially to the poor. The "poor" (*ptochoi*) has the literal meaning of those who crouch, the people who cringe, and the ones who are bent from the weight of need. The word belongs to the root *pte*, crouched together (see also: *ptesse*, be afraid; *ptosse*, lower one's head in fear; *ptox*, timid). In its figurative meaning, *ptochoi* are the beggarly poor, the economically destitute, those who are utterly dependent on the help of strangers. That understanding is carried into the New Testament, where the poor are those who are bent over and heavily burdened: widows, orphans, the handicapped, the lost, the unemployed, the overlooked, the helpless, anyone who is at the mercy of others or punishing circumstances. In a parable of the kingdom, Luke lists them as "the poor, the maimed, the lame, and the blind" (14:21).

These are the marginal people in every society. Everything would be fine, people say, but for "them". In the Gospel the "them" of society become the "us" of the kingdom – the lost and the last and the least, whose open woundedness is a cry to the graciousness of God. These are the ones who are hugged into importance by an eccentric king who cherishes them above all others. These are the ones who are surprised by love and beneficence in the parables of the kingdom.

FURTHER READING

J. Fuellenbach,	*Throw Fire* (Manila: Logos, 1998) pp.69-78; 239-260; *The Kingdom of God* (Manila: Logos, 1993)
J.P. Meier,	*A Marginal Jew,* Vol. 2 pp. 237-454
J. Riches,	"Jesus and his kingdom" in *The World of Jesus* (Cambridge: Cambridge University Press, 1991) pp. 108-125
P. Perkins,	*Jesus as Teacher* (Cambridge: Cambridge University Press, 1991) pp. 38-61
J. Weiss,	*Jesus' Proclamation of the Kingdom of God* (London: SCM, 1971)
L. Wostyn,	*Doing Christology* (Manila: Claretian, 1990) pp. 143-161
N. Perrin,	*Jesus and the Language of the Kingdom* (Philadelphia: Fortress, 1975)
J. Sobrino,	*Jesus the Liberator* (New York: Orbis Books, 1993)

REFLECTION: THE KINGDOM
BY R.S. THOMAS

It's a long way off but inside it
There are quite different things going on:
Festivals at which the poor man
Is king and the consumptive is
Healed; mirrors in which the blind look
At themselves and love looks at them
Back; and industry is for mending
The bent bones and the minds fractured
By life. It's a long way off, but to get
There takes no time and admission
Is free, if you will purge yourself
Of desire, and present yourself with
Your need only and the simple offering
Of your faith, green as a leaf.

R.S. Thomas, Collected Poems 1945–1990 *(London: Phoenix, 1996) p.233*

23 THE PARABLES AND THE KINGDO.

Why do we tell stories? To entertain; to instruct; to defend; to criticise; to confuse; to subvert etc. Different kinds of stories have different purposes. Traditionally there are five types of story, each with a different goal.

story types	myth	apologue	action	satire	parable
The story's relationship to the world beyond the story	establishes the world by foundational stories of opposites: human/divine life/death male/female good/bad. Reconciling the opposites.	defends the world by persuading people of its truth; these stories attempt to reinforce people's cherished convictions.	investigates the world by presenting contrasting characters about whose fates we care. Usually resolved by conclusion.	attacks the world by ridiculing pretentious people and institutions; these stories attempt to expose hypocrisy.	subverts the world by exposing oppression and selfishness; these stories attempt to introduce new values.
Examples	Creation stories	The Tales of Aesop	Most novels and films	Political cartoons	Rich man and Lazarus

One of the interesting marks of Jesus' ministry is how much of his teaching is done through storytelling. Strangely for us, Jesus communicates his most telling truths through the medium of short narrative fiction in the form of parable. He invites his hearers to use their imagination and follow him into the world of parable. He hopes that his listeners will see things differently, so that when they leave the world of parable for the world of their experience, they will return with new insight. The parables are a challenge to change.

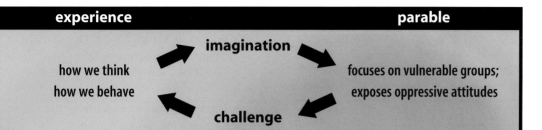

experience		parable

imagination

how we think
how we behave

focuses on vulnerable groups;
exposes oppressive attitudes

challenge

1) How do you challenge people to change? How do you confront people who see things differently? How do you communicate the contrary way you see things?

The answer to these questions depends largely on your cultural tradition and personality. In some traditions it is acceptable to confront people directly and unambiguously: you name what is wrong, you "tell it like it is". In other traditions this direct approach is regarded as crude and harmful to relationships: instead, the confrontation is done indirectly, either through the medium of go-betweens or through the medium of indirect language. The parable is a way of confronting people indirectly: it uses the medium of fiction to encode what is wrong and to explore new possibility. Using the parable to introduce new thinking is one of the ways Jesus exercises his own pastoral leadership.

2) In the parables what is contrasted is not this world versus another different world: what is contrasted is different ways of living within the world. In the Parable of the Prodigal Son, for example, two different ways of responding to failure and sin are explored. The father runs to be gracious; the elder son cannot move to mercy. Both characters belong to the same world, the same race, the same tribe, and the same family. But only one of them shows the radical values of the kingdom within their shared world. The contrast is not between worlds; it is between different ways of being in the same world. Thus the parables are sacred in our tradition as a way of calling us to live out Jesus' values within our own world.

3) In Jesus' parables there is a marked absence of the supernatural: most parables are realistic fictions. Jesus baptises the ordinary and tells us that it is in the theatre of the ordinary that the drama of the kingdom is being lived out. By calling on everyday experience, the parables tell us that we are saved where we are. In the parables we are invited to make a choice and come to a decision; they invite us to pay attention, come alive and face things. The parables leave us wondering about our own reactions: they tease us to reflect again on attitudes and behaviour we take for granted.

4) Behind the parable there is the challenge to repent. The word repent comes from the Greek: *meta/noia* or across/think.

It literally means to think across the way we normally think; to change our outlook; to change our minds about things. The eternal challenge of the parables, therefore, is to question what we take for granted. In that sense the parable makes us uncomfortable: it invites us to borrow the eyes of Jesus and look at ourselves, others and the world in a new light. In the same way, the parables can

Solomon Saprid:
(Philippines) The Return

be seen to be subversive, because they use the medium of fiction to challenge the way things are – e.g. the Parable of the Wicked Tenants in Mark 12:1-12. This illustrates clearly how dangerous it is for Jesus to use parable as a way of criticising authority.

5) The word parable comes from the Greek root *para/bole* or beside/throw.

When Jesus speaks about the kingdom, he never says what the kingdom actually is, he says only what it is like. Jesus borrows images and drama from the people and countryside around him. He is not an uncritical observer of what he sees. He uses what he observes, names what is wrong, and proposes another way. His other way tries to catch something of the unseen reality of the kingdom of God.

FURTHER READING

R. Longnecker (ed.),	*The Challenge of Jesus' Parables* (Michigan: Eerdmans, 2000)
D. McBride,	*The Parables of Jesus* (Chawton: Redemptorist Publications, 1999)
W.R. Herzog,	*Parables as Subversive Speech* (Louisville: Westminster, 1995)
B.B. Scott,	*Hear Then the Parable* (Philadelphia: Fortress, 1990)
N. Fisher,	*The Parables of Jesus* (New York: Crossroad, 1990)
J. Drury,	*The Parables in the Gospels* (London: SPCK, 1985)
K. Bailey,	*Poet & Peasant and Through Peasant Eyes* (Michigan: Eerdmans, 1983)
A.N. Wilder,	*Jesus' Parables and the War of Myths* (London: SPCK, 1982)
S. TeSelle,	*Speaking in Parables* (Philadelphia: Fortress, 1975)
J.D. Crossan,	*In Parables* (New York: Harper & Row, 1973)
J. Jeremias,	*The Parables of Jesus* (London: SCM, 1972)
D. Via,	*The Parables* (Philadelphia: Fortress, 1967)
C.H. Dodd,	*The Parables of the Kingdom* (London: Collins, 1967)

THE PARABLES IN THE GOSPELS

	MARK	MATTHEW	LUKE	JOHN
1. New cloth on old	2:21	9:16	5:36	
2. New wine in old wineskins	2:22	9:17	5:37-39	
3. The sower	4:1-9	13:1-9	8:4-8	
4. A light under a bushel	4:21-23	5:14-16	8:16-17	
5. The seed that grows secretly	4:26-29			
6. The mustard seed	4:30-32	13:31-32	13:18-19	
7. The wicked tenants	12:1-9	21:33-46	20:9-19	
8. Fig tree as herald of summer	13:28-29	24:32-33	21:29-31	
9. Salt		5:13		
10. Houses on rock and on sand		7:24-27	6:47-49	
11. The weeds in the field		13:24-30, 36-43		
12. The leaven		13:33	13:20-21	
13. Hidden treasure		13:44		
14. Pearl of great value		13:45-46		
15. Drag-net		13:47-50		
16. Lost sheep		18:12-14	15:1-7	
17. Unforgiving slave		18:23-35		
18. Workers in the vineyard		20:1-16		
19. Two sons		21:28-31		
20. Wedding feast		22:1-14		
21. Ten maidens		25:1-13		
22. Talents		25:14-30		
23. Last judgement		25:31-46		
24. Faithful servant		25:45:51		
25. Creditor and the debtors			7:41-43	
26. Good Samaritan			10:25-37	
27. Friend at midnight			11:5-8	
28. Rich fool			12:13-21	
29. Alert servants			12:35-40	
30. Fig tree without figs			13:6-9	
31. Places of honour at the wedding feast			14:7-14	
32. Great feast			14:15-24	
33. Counting the cost			14:28-33	
34. Lost coin			15:8-10	
35. Prodigal son			15:11-32	
36. Unjust slave			16:1-8	
37. Rich man and Lazarus			16:19-31	
38. The master and his servant			17:7-10	
39. Unjust judge			18:1-8	
40. The Pharisee and the tax collector			18:9-14	
41. Gold coins			19:11-27	

THE MIRACLES OF JESUS

1) By what authority?

The inbreaking of the kingdom of God is illustrated in the Gospels by Jesus' activity: "He has done all things well; he even makes the deaf hear and the dumb speak" (Mk 7:37). Strangely, the Greek word for miracle, *thauma*, appears nowhere in the Gospels; they only say that the mighty acts and signs of Jesus aroused surprise and amazement. The word "miracle" derives from the Latin *mirari*, "to wonder at".

The New Testament accounts of miracles are not unique in the Graeco-Roman world. What makes them different is the divine reference: they attribute the extraordinary phenomenon reported, not to deities or polytheism, but to the one God of Israel and/or his agents, Jesus or his followers.

When people think of miracles today, it usually refers to human achievement, e.g. "He has made a miraculous recovery". When Christians talk of Jesus' miracles, we often think of events that contradict the laws of nature or are proofs of Jesus' divinity. These categories, however, are strangers in the Gospel tradition. The concept of a law of nature – as opposed to a law of God – was alien to the people in the ancient world: nature already was the creation of God. And if Jesus' miracles are a proof of his divinity, it makes strange sense for Jesus to instruct his disciples to do exactly what he has done: "Heal the sick, raise the dead, cleanse lepers, cast out demons" (Mt 10:8).

Earlier in the Gospel Matthew shows people coming to Jesus, among them some who are noted for casting out demons and "working many miracles in your name" (7:22). These people are rejected as evil men. Clearly, working miracles, even in the name of Jesus, cannot be *automatically* interpreted as a sign of goodness. False prophets can work signs and wonders (Mk 13:22).

In the Gospel accounts miracles provoke a faith-filled recognition of the wondrous graciousness of God or suggest the presence of the prince of darkness, Beelzebub.

The problem in the Gospels is not about Jesus performing mighty works – many other people do that. The question is *by what authority does Jesus do what he does?* Is Jesus "of God" or "of the devil"? The miracles, therefore, do not provide a ready answer to the question: "Who is this man?" 'Rather the miracles provoke the question: "Who is this man who…?" The verb that qualifies "this man" questions the identity of the subject of the action.

2) Binding evil and unbinding people

The central question in the Gospel is interpreting Jesus in the light of what he does and says. Is his activity a sign of his closeness to God or to the evil one? If the world of the Gospel interpreted illness – especially mental illness – as being in the power of the evil one, Jesus is seen to confront that power with his more powerful benevolence. There is a clash of two kingdoms.

What Jesus does is seen by the evil powers as an act of aggression – like the healing of the Gerasene demoniac in Luke 8:26-39. The power of God in Jesus liberates a man who has been made to suffer at the hands of the evil one. (The devils are deceived and, via the pigs, are dismissed from the story.) The man's community rejects Jesus and he departs, as if to demonstrate that he can do little for those who do not trust him. But Jesus does not reject the community: he tells the healed man to return to them and proclaim **what God has done**. The man responds by proclaiming throughout the whole town **what Jesus has done**. Again, the real question is: given what has happened, who then is Jesus?

Similarly in the story of the healing of the man born blind in John 9: the focus rests not on the identity of the one who is healed but on the identity of the one who heals: "The man said, 'Lord, I believe', and worshipped him" (Jn 9:8).

3) Miracles and Jesus' identity

a) Jesus' acts of power are gracious responses to the concrete needs of people, and he refuses to supply signs to legitimise his prophetic authority: "Why does this generation seek a sign? Truly, I say to you, no sign shall be given it" (Mk 8:11-12). Jesus refuses to legitimise his ministry with signs, not least because they will not answer the problem they are expected to solve. Does one blind man believe because another blind man receives his sight? Since false prophets can perform signs and mighty acts (Mk 13: 21-23), clearly the question of legitimacy is not answered by the acts themselves.

b) Jesus does not work miracles for display, for his own advancement or comfort, for money, or to punish. In his healing miracles he identifies himself with people in fear and distress and hurt, in order to release and restore them: that is his identity.

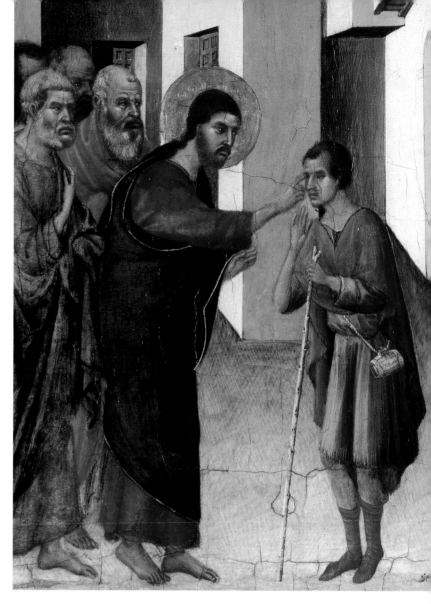

Duccio:

Jesus Opens the Eyes of a Man Born Blind (detail)

c) The nature miracles – like the stilling of the storm (Mk 4:35-41) – display a different purpose from Jesus' concern for afflicted people. Their focus in the narrative is clearly on the little faith of those who followed the historical Jesus: "Why are you so afraid? Do you still not believe?" Genuine faith would make the miracle unnecessary; and the disciples do not come to belief in Jesus, anyway, because of a miracle during the ministry. *The miracle leads them into a question: "Who is this man?"* Again, the focus is on the identity of Jesus.

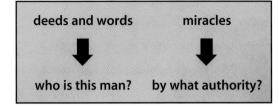

deeds and words	miracles
⬇	⬇
who is this man?	by what authority?

4) Miracles: a growth industry?

"Literary criticism reveals a tendency to intensify, magnify and multiply the miracles. According to Mark 1:34, Jesus healed many sick; in the parallel Matthew 8:16 he heals them all. In Mark, Jairus' daughter is on the point of death; in Matthew she is already dead. The healing of one blind man and one possessed become the healing of two blind men and two possessed. The feeding of the 4000 becomes the feeding of the 5000, and the seven baskets left over become twelve. If this tendency to develop, multiply and intensify can be found in the Gospels themselves, then naturally it must also be presumed to have existed in the period before the Gospels were compiled."

(W. Kasper, Jesus the Christ, *p. 89)*

The Gospels themselves reveal a growth industry when it comes to reporting miracles, keen as they are to illustrate their Easter proclamation about Jesus. While the historical Jesus left behind him a powerful memory of miracle working, as well as an embarrassing memory that in Nazareth he could perform no mighty works (Mk 6:5), clearly the tradition has been extended and magnified. Granted this, the development still offers statements of faith about the significance of Jesus and the salvation he continues to bring.

5) Exegesis of three example miracle stories

a) **An exorcism:** The Gerasene demoniac (Mk 5:1–20; Lk 8:26–39; Mt 8:28–34)

b) **A nature miracle:** Jesus stilling the storm (Mk 4:35–41; Lk 8:22–25; Mt 8:23–27)

c) **A healing and more:** The daughter of Jairus (Mk 5:21–43; Lk 8:40–56; Mt 9:18–26)

FURTHER READING

J. Pilch,	*Healing in the New Testament: Insights from Medical and Mediterranean Anthropology* (Philadelphia: Fortress Press, 2000)
J.P. Meier,	"Miracles" in *A Marginal Jew: Rethinking the Historical Jesus* (1994) pp. 509–970
W. Kasper,	"Jesus' miracles" in *Jesus the Christ* (London: Burns & Oates, 1977) pp. 89–99
E. Schillebeeckx,	*Jesus* pp. 179–200
J. Jeremias,	*New Testament Theology,* Vol. 1 (London: SCM 1971) pp. 85–96
J. Rhymer,	*The Miracles of Jesus* (Slough: St Paul's, 1991)
J. Fitzmyer,	"Satan and Demons in Luke-Acts" in *Luke the Theologian* pp 146–169
H. Hendrickx,	*The Miracles of Jesus* (London: Chapman, 1987)
D. Senior,	"Jesus Heals" in *Jesus: A Gospel Portrait* (New York: Paulist, 1992) pp. 100–116

THE MIRACLES IN THE GOSPELS

H = healing   E = exorcism   R = raising from dead   N = nature

	MARK	MATTHEW	LUKE	JOHN
1. The demoniac in the synagogue (E)	1:23-26		4:31-37	
2. Peter's mother-in-law (H)	1:29-31	8:14-15	4:38-39	
3. Many possessed (E)	1:32-34	8:16-17	4:40-41	
4. An individual leper (H)	1:40-45	8:2-4	5:12-16	
5. The paralysed man (H)	2:1-12	9:2-8	5:17-26	
6. The man with a withered hand (H)	3:1-6	12:9-13	6:6-11	
7. Stilling the storm (N)	4:35-41	8:23-27	8:22-25	
8. The Gerasene demoniac (E)	5:1-20	8:28-34	8:26-39	
9. Jairus' daughter (R)	5:22-24, 35-43	9:18-19, 23-25	8:41-42, 49-56	
10. The woman with a haemorrhage (H)	5:25-34	9:20-22	8:43-48	
11. Feeding the 5,000 (N)	6:31-44	14:13-21	9:10-17	6:1-15
12. Walking on the water (N)	6:45-52	14:22-33		6:16-21
13. The Syro-Phoenician woman (E)	7:24-30	15:21-28		
14. The deaf-mute (H)	7:31-37			
15. Feeding the 4,000 (N)	8:1-10	15:32-39		
16. The centurion's servant/son (H)	8:5-13		7:1-10	4:46-53
17. The blind man at Bethsaida (H)	8:22-26			
18. The possessed boy (E)	9:14-29	17:14-21	9:37-43	
19. The mute demoniac (E)	9:32-34		11:14-15	
20. Bartimaeus/the blind man of Jericho/(H)	10:46-52	20:29-34	18:35-43	
21. The withered fig tree (N)	11:12-14, 20-24	21:18-22		
22. Two blind men (H)		9:27-31		
23. The mute and blind demoniac (E)		12:22-24	11:14	
24. The coin in the fish's mouth (N)		17:24-27		
25. Simon Peter and a catch of fish (N)			5:1-11	21:1-11
26. The son of the widow of Nain (R)			7:11-17	
27. The woman bent double (H)			13:10-13	
28. The man with dropsy (H)			14:1-6	
29. The ten lepers (H)			17:11-19	
30. The high priest's slave (H)			22:50-51	
31. The wedding at Cana (N)				2:1-11
32. The sick man at Pool of Bethesda (H)				5:1-9
33. The man blind from birth (H)				9:1-41
34. Lazarus (R)				11:1-44

JESUS AND TABLE FELLOWSHIP

1) Jesus' mission statement

One of the things Jesus regularly did throughout his ministry was to eat with tax collectors and sinners, an activity that caused genuine offence to many of his contemporaries. This pastoral activity clearly set Jesus apart from both John the Baptist and the Pharisees. Jesus' mission and the one he offers to his disciples can be summarised as follows:

- **For himself:** *"I am sent only to the lost sheep of the house of Israel."* (Mt 15:24)

- **For the disciples:** 1st – *"Go only to the lost sheep of the house of Israel."* (Mt 10:6)
2nd – *"Go, make disciples of all nations…"* (Mt 28:19)

> *"'Sinners' in the Hebrew Bible, when used generically to refer to a class of people, refers not to those who occasionally transgress, but to those who are outside the law in some fundamental way. To understand the significance of the term 'sinners', we should consider the description of the 'wicked' in the Psalms. They are contrasted with the 'poor'. The wicked prey on the poor, and they say in their hearts that there is no God, or if there is he will not call them to account (Pss. 10.4, 8-13). Modern English translations of the Hebrew Psalms quite rightly use the word 'wicked' in these passages, which is the best translation of the Hebrew word resha'im. The Jews who translated the Hebrew Bible into Greek, however, used the word 'sinners' (hamartoloi), and this became the term that Greek-speaking Jews used for people who were fundamentally outside the covenant because they did not observe God's law… The significance of the fact that Jesus was a friend of the wicked was this: he counted within his fellowship people who were generally regarded as living outside the law in a blatant manner."*
>
> (E.P. Sanders, The Historical Figure of Jesus (London: Allen Lane, 1993), p.227)

2) Sacred space and ordinary space

Given his declared mission, how does Jesus fulfil the task he has set himself? Jesus answers the question, one that we all have to answer in our ministry, about what enables people to change. What do you think helps people to change? Different religious groups will answer that question differently. At some

Sacred Space		Ordinary Space
Temple		Wilderness
Sacrificial Altar	**John the Baptist**	River Jordan
Synagogue		Open Air
(Church)		Seashore
(Mosque)		Hillside
(Convent)		Villages — **Jesus**
(Monastery)		Houses
		Table

point in his ministry, Jesus makes the decision that the best way to help people to change is to connect with them, associate with them, and eat with them. We take this so much for granted that we forget how radical it is. Jesus is not going to stay in the desert; he is not going to wait until people seek him out. He makes a decision that his ministry is going to go into people's lives: he goes where people live and gather, to the towns and villages, to the market-places; he goes into their houses, he sits at their tables, and he uses the table as his place of ministry. If you believe that you have a ministry and at the same time the hierarchy forbids you to use their territory – the synagogue or the church or the mosque – how are you going to reach people? What is your forum going to be? That depends on your mission statement. If you want to reach "the lost", where do you find them?

For John the Baptist, the principal space of his ministry was the wilderness of Judea and the River Jordan. Jesus makes a decision that his sanctuary, his sacred place, is not going to be the synagogue and certainly not the Temple, because by the end of his career he damns the Temple and the whole Temple organisation, warning that it is going to be destroyed (Mk 11:12-21). Instead of operating in sacred space, Jesus decides to reach out to people where they live and work. Jesus has a genius for using what is ordinary and making it sacred.

The movement away from sacred space is summarised by the Fourth Evangelist in the exchange between Jesus and the woman of Samaria:

"'Our fathers worshipped on this mountain, while you say that Jerusalem is the place where one ought to worship.' Jesus said: 'Believe me, woman, the hour is coming when you will worship the Father neither on this mountain nor in Jerusalem… The hour will

come – in fact it is here already – when true worshippers will worship the Father in spirit and truth.'" (Jn 4:20-23)

Sacred space – temples, cathedrals, churches, pagodas, mosques, synagogues – are often the most beautiful buildings in towns and cities, standing as architectural testimonies to people's cherished beliefs and values. They can also, however, become the focus of people's protest.

Basilica of St Francis, Assisi

"Whenever Christians want to rebel against the organized Church with its hierarchies and traditions, against the prestige inherent in beautiful buildings, against having to fit into structures instead of feeling free to create and expand into the new – then they tend to complain about churches. After a while, if they continue to meet at all, they prefer bare halls, basements, living rooms, and garages in which to pray together: in these they feel they are being purer, more energetic, approaching closer to their roots. It is a true and faithful option, and often a necessary one for those who choose it."

(Margaret Visser, The Geometry of Love: Space, Time, Mystery and Meaning in an Ordinary Church *(Canada: HarperFlamingo, 2000) p.125)*

3) *A unique mark of Jesus' ministry*

One of the most vivid memories associated with the historical Jesus is his table fellowship, a unique mark of his ministry that distinguished him clearly from John the Baptist and the Pharisees: ***"And they said to him, 'The disciples of John fast often and offer prayers, and so do the disciples of the Pharisees; but yours go on eating and drinking.' And Jesus said to them 'Can you make wedding guests fast while the bridegroom is with them?'"*** (Lk 5:33-34).

For the disciples, the presence of Jesus means freedom from fasting and mourning. Jesus does not limit table fellowship to his own followers but extends it to everyone, including sinners, a practice forbidden among Jews. Such is Jesus' habit that his opponents will call him "a glutton and a drunkard, a friend of taxcollectors and sinners" (Lk 7:34). What Jesus' opponents believe to be irreligious practice becomes Jesus' regular religious activity.

Jesus eats with the rich and the poor, tax collectors and Zealots, Pharisees and sinners: he has a truly catholic taste for table companions, making him the most indiscriminate host in biblical tradition. His radical belief is that **unrestricted table fellowship and indiscriminate welcome are the best ways of bringing salvation to people,** especially to those who are excluded from the Temple and the tables of the righteous. And since he believes that the kingdom of God looks like a magnificent feast for the legion of the unwanted, Jesus displays God's unique style in the present tense. Jesus wants the unwanted; he loves the unloved; he has a passion to break bread with broken people. The best way he shows all this is by welcoming sinners and eating with them.

Pastoral strategies for change: what enables people to change?		
John the Baptist	**The Pharisees**	**Jesus**
belief in God as Judge preaching the kingdom fasting & prayer baptism for sinners	belief in God as Judge fidelity to Law & tradition fasting & prayer segregation from sinners	belief in God as Father preaching the kingdom prayer to 'Abba' association with sinners
↓	↓	↓
conversion & forgiveness	conversion & forgiveness	table fellowship & forgiveness
↓	↓	↓
avoidance of retribution	table fellowship	conversion

4) Table fellowship: a goal or a means?

Both Jesus and the Pharisees believed in fellowship meals. The Pharisees believed, like many others, that sharing a meal was a covenant experience. The meals made commemorated the sacred covenant, "You will be my people, and I will be your God" (see Ex 19:5-6). Thus rites of purification surrounded the meal: hands had to be washed, utensils had to be purified, and the food had to be carefully chosen. That care was reflected in those who were invited to a meal. According to the Babylonian Talmud, upright people would never accept an invitation to a meal, unless they could identify with approval the other guests. *If these meals were moments of communion for the upright, they were also moments of separation for outsiders. Selectivity always involves discrimination.*

An ancient Scottish blessing, greeting the guest on arrival, deliberately avoids enquiring about the identity of the guest – he or she might come from an enemy clan – postponing mutual revelation until the meal itself is under way:

"Hail Guest, we ask not what thou art.
If friend, we greet thee, hand on heart.
If stranger, such no longer be.
If foe, our love shall conquer thee."

For the Pharisees, sharing a meal was a way of celebrating the covenant with God and with those who shared in the blessings of God. To break bread with others was to accept them, to offer them fellowship, to honour them, to make a sanctuary for them, to share life with them. To share your table with the unholy and unclean would be an openly sacrilegious act. Conversion for the Pharisees, therefore, was a necessary condition for communion.

Jesus' genius is to reverse the sequence: he uses the meal *as a way of coming to fellowship with*

him prior to conversion. Zacchaeus' conversion, for example, is not a condition for eating with Jesus; rather, eating with Jesus is what makes for Zacchaeus' change. Jesus' method is built on respect rather than threat: in associating with sinners, Jesus is clearly affirming their basic worth – which is why the Pharisees and scribes object so strongly.

Jesus does not believe that making people feel like moral lepers is likely to lead to their conversion; it is far more likely to confirm them in moral paralysis.

Love and forgiveness are offered in the hope that change and renewal will be the result; they are not the *reward* for conversion. Thus, meals with Jesus are a graced opportunity for renewal – something that is manifestly true even of the final meal, the Last Supper, where the palpable hope is that – even at this late stage – destructive plans might be averted.

Sadao Watanabe:
The Last Supper (Japan)

5) Acting out images of God

The sequence of forgiveness leading to conversion is celebrated in the book of Wisdom. Not surprisingly, the insight begins with the image of a merciful God:

"You are merciful to all because you can do all things and overlook men's sins so that they can repent. Yes, you love all that exists, you hold nothing of what you have made in abhorrence, for had you hated anything, you would not have formed it... You spare all things because all things are yours, Lord, lover of life... Little by little, therefore, you correct those who offend... So that they may abstain from evil and trust in you, Lord."

(Wis 11:22-12:2)

6) Jesus' pastoral strategy, like everyone else's, emerges from his image of God. We act out of the way we imagine God. Jesus' readiness to forgive, to break bread, to seek out those who live beyond the boundaries of religious and social approval – all this is commentary on *the kind of God* he believes in. When his preference for the outcast meets with the outrage of the righteous, Jesus confronts the religious values of his opponents.

By cherishing the people his opponents despise, Jesus calls into question the value system that allows religious people to rubbish others and the kind of God that supports that destructive attitude.

There are some people who adopt what they are pleased to call a muscular moral stance on certain people and issues, but their attitudes are indistinguishable from religious snobbery. This is why Jesus challenged those "who prided themselves on being virtuous and despised everyone else" (Lk 18:9).

7) Jesus' open table fellowship is celebrated in many of his parables: for example

"Go out to the highways and byways and compel people to come in, that my house may be filled." (Lk 14:23)

"And the servants went out into the streets and gathered all whom they found, the good and the bad alike; so the wedding hall was filled with guests." (Mt 22:10)

The above scenes, which Jesus offers as insights into the kingdom of God, would be most people's social nightmare: an uncensored mix of people gathering at table to eat together. There is no social hierarchy, no division of the sexes or classes, no discrimination, no power gathering. It paints a picture of what the Irish writer Edna O'Brien said was needed for a good dinner table: "A mixture of magic and anarchy." This is contrary to the practice of most societies, where who is invited to table is defined by group boundaries, custom, propriety, etc.

"In all societies, both simple and complex, eating is the primary way of initiating and maintaining human relationships... Once the anthropologist finds out where, when, and with whom the food is eaten, just about everything else can be inferred about the relations among the society's members... To know what, where, how, when, and with whom people eat is to know the character of their society."

(P. Farb and G Armelagos, Consuming Passions: The Anthropology of Eating *(Boston: Houghton Miffin, 1980) pp. 4, 211)*

The open and egalitarian table fellowship that Jesus advocated provides a map for his kingdom. If the table is a miniature of society, then Jesus' table fellowship is a miniature of his kingdom. But what he shares as his dream is what so many others fear as dishonourable and chaotic, confused and anarchic. On the subject of indiscriminate table fellowship, Jesus is alone among his contemporaries; and in this matter, sadly, it seems that he still remains alone.

FURTHER READING

P. Simons,   "Jesus' Table Companionship" – a series of 10 articles published in *Spirituality*, throughout the issues 1999-2000

J.D. Crossan,   *Jesus: a Revolutionary Biography* (San Francisco: Harper, 1994) pp.54-74

F. Moloney,   *A Body Broken for a Broken People* (Manila: Claretian, 1990) pp. 121-137

P. Bernier,   *Bread Broken and Shared* (Indiana: Ave Maria, 1981)

REFLECTION: TABLE FELLOWSHIP; SACRED SPACE
PARIS BY PAUL MULDOON

A table for two will scarcely seat
The pair of us! All the people we have been
Are here as guests, strategically deployed
As to who will go best with whom,
A convent girl, a crashing bore, the couple

Who aren't quite all they seem.
A last shrimp curls and winces on your plate
Like an embryo. "Is that a little overdone?"
And these country faces at the window
That were once our own. They study the menu,

Smile faintly, and are gone.
Chicken Marengo! It's a far cry from the Moy.
"There's no such person as Saint Christopher,
Father Talbot gave it out at Mass,
Same as there's no such place as Limbo."

The world's less simple for being travelled,
Though. In each fresh neutral place
Where our differences might have been settled
There were men sitting down to talk of peace
Who began with the shape of the table.

B. Morrison & A. Motion (ed), **Contemporary British Poetry** *(Harmondsworth: Penguin, 1972) pp.140–141*

REFLECTION: CHURCH GOING
BY PHILIP LARKIN (EXCERPT)

Once I am sure there's nothing going on
I step inside, letting the door thud shut.
Another church: matting, seats, and stone,
And little books; sprawlings of flowers, cut
For Sunday, brownish now; some brass and stuff
Up at the holy end; the small neat organ;
And a tense, musty, unignorable silence,
Brewed God knows how long. Hatless, I take off
My cycle-clips in awkward reverence,

Move forward, run my hand around the font.
From where I stand, the roof looks almost new –
Cleaned, or restored? Someone would know: I don't.
Mounting the lectern, I peruse a few
Hectoring large-scale verses, and pronounce
'Here endeth' much more loudly than I'd meant.
The echoes snigger briefly. Back at the door
I sign the book, donate an Irish sixpence,
Reflect the place was not worth stopping for.

Yet stop I did: in fact I often do,
And always end much at a loss like this,
Wondering what to look for; wondering, too,
When churches fall completely out of use
What we shall turn them into, if we shall keep
A few cathedrals chronically on show,
Their parchment, plate and pyx in locked cases,
And let the rest rent-free to rain and sheep.
Shall we avoid them as unlucky places?

…

A serious house on serious earth it is,
In whose blent air all our compulsions meet,
Are recognised, and robed as destinies.
And that much never can be obsolete,
Since someone will forever be surprising
A hunger in himself to be more serious,
And gravitating with it to this ground,
Which, he once heard, was proper to grow wise in,
If only that so many dead lie round.

P. Larkin, The Less Deceived (London: Marvell Press, 1985) pp.29-30

26 AT THE TABLE OF SIMON THE PHARISEE (LUKE 7:36-50)

Jesus uses the table as a place for teaching, for confronting, for healing, for forgiveness. Explore the differences between the attitude of Jesus and Simon towards an uninvited woman who appears among the dinner guests. Where is the source of conflict? Who is in conflict with whom? What is the issue?

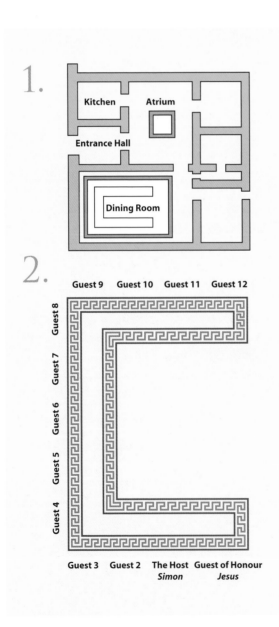

1.

Kitchen   Atrium

Entrance Hall

Dining Room

2.

Guest 9   Guest 10   Guest 11   Guest 12

Guest 8
Guest 7
Guest 6
Guest 5
Guest 4

Guest 3   Guest 2   The Host   Guest of Honour
                   Simon   Jesus

1. The house

To the left is the ground-floor plan of the Villa Anaploga in Corinth, first-century. It represents the typical layout of a rich person's house in the Roman empire of that time. Usually the ground floor consisted of reception rooms, while the family's bedrooms were located upstairs, ensuring privacy. Central to the house was the atrium where family and visitors could gather; the dining room consisted of a triclinium: literally, three sides for leaning, where guests would recline at table. It was in houses like this that the early eucharist was celebrated (see 1 Cor 11:17-22).

2. The triclinium – the three-sided arrangement for reclining on couches at table

At a formal dinner, the host would be positioned in such a way that the guest of honour would be to his right, while the other guests would go around the three sides in hierarchical order. (See Jesus' advice on taking positions at table in Luke 14:7-11.)

3. If you were a guest at a banquet given by a rich householder, usually you were offered four signs of hospitality:

a) The offering of peace/kiss of greeting: This was to honour with a blessing those who graced the house. In the Roman tradition, two empty weapon hands were shaken as a pledge of peace.

b) The anointing with oil: Originally oil was poured on the king's head on the day he was crowned. Following the demise of the monarchy, oil was used for healing the sick and for consecrating priests and objects for worship. With the collapse of royalty the psalmists looked for the day when the *Christos*, the anointed one, would come. The act of pouring oil on the head became a way of welcoming guests. "You spread the table before me in the sight of my foes; you anoint my head with oil; my cup overflows" (see Ps 23). "How good and pleasant it is, people dwelling in community. Like precious oil on the head, running down the beard of Aaron, running down over the collar of his robe" (See Ps 133).

c) The washing of the feet: Washing the feet of the guest: see Abraham in Genesis 18:4. In John's Gospel Jesus turns this act of hospitality into a sacred rite (Jn 13).

d) The meal: This was the principal act of hospitality, and was sometimes seen as an encounter with the divine (Gen 18:1-5; Ex 24:9-11). Throughout his ministry Jesus uses the meal as a sign of God's indiscriminate welcome, particularly to sinners, just as at the end of his life he asks his followers to remember him by celebrating a meal: "Do this in memory of me."

4. Immediately following Luke's recitation of a comparison between Jesus' ministry and that of John the Baptist (Lk 7:31-35) – distinguishing Jesus as the one who eats and drinks with people – the evangelist recounts his story of a woman who comes to anoint Jesus Luke portrays the differences between the attitude of Jesus and Simon towards this uninvited woman who appears among the dinner guests.

Nicolas Poussin:

Sacrament of Penance

In Nicolas Poussin's painting, Sacrament of Penance, completed in 1647, the artist chose the dinner at Simon's house as his biblical scene to depict Penance in his series of seven sacraments. The triclinium is well represented; Jesus is sitting in the correct place of the guest of honour, but Poussin has moved Simon across the table from Jesus, for obvious dramatic effect. While a male servant is washing Simon's feet, Jesus' feet are being washed by the tears of the uninvited woman, whom everyone in the room can easily identify as a sinner. Her hair, as tradition demands, is bound up, but that will soon change in the development of the story.

While Simon offers Jesus one sign of hospitality, the meal, the woman offers Jesus three: the kiss; the washing of the feet; the anointing.

Jesus first ministers to Simon indirectly, through the medium of fiction, using parable to confront his host about his attitude to the uninvited woman.

Jesus compares two responses: the loving extravagance of the woman and the arctic propriety of the host.

Luke 7:36–50

"One of the Pharisees invited him to a meal. When he arrived at the Pharisee's house and took his place at table, a woman came in, who had a bad name in the town. She had heard he was dining with the Pharisee and had brought with her an alabaster jar of ointment. She waited behind him at his feet, weeping, and her tears fell on his feet, and she wiped them away with her hair; then she covered his feet with kisses and anointed them with the ointment. When the Pharisee who had invited him saw this, he said to himself, 'If this man were a prophet, he would know who this woman is that is touching him and what a bad name she has.'

"Then Jesus took him up and said, 'Simon, I have something to say to you'. 'Speak, Master,' was the reply. 'There was once a creditor who had two men in his debt; one owed him five hundred denarii, the other fifty. They were unable to pay, so he pardoned them both. Which of them will love him more?' 'The one who was pardoned more, I suppose,' answered Simon. Jesus said, 'You are right.'

"Then he turned to the woman. 'Simon,' he said, 'do you see this woman? I came into your house, and you poured no water over my feet, but she has poured out her tears over my feet and wiped them away with her hair. You gave me no kiss, but she has been covering my feet with kisses ever since I came in. You did not anoint my head with oil, but she has anointed my feet with ointment. For this reason I tell you that her sins, her many sins, must have been forgiven her, or she would not have shown such great love. It is the man who is forgiven little who shows little love.' Then he said to her, 'Your sins are forgiven.' Those who were with him at table began to say to themselves, 'Who is this man, that he even forgives sins?' But he said to the woman, 'Your faith has saved you; go in peace.'"

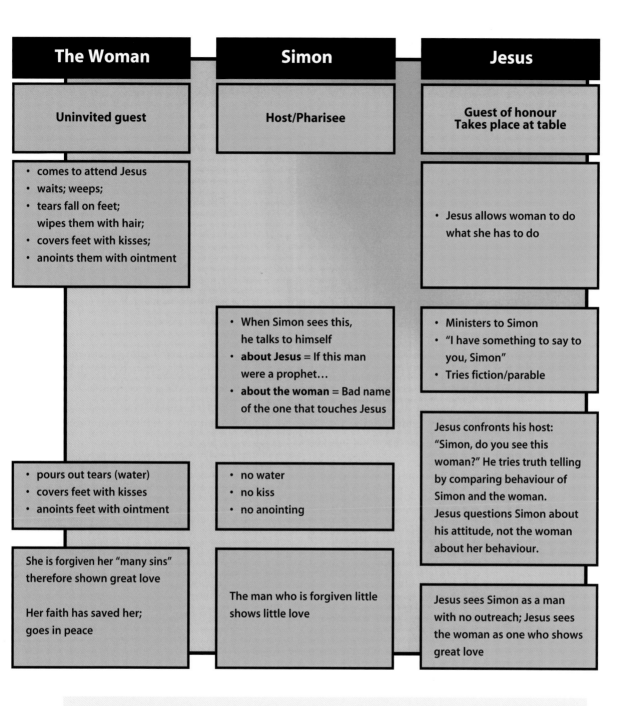

The Woman	Simon	Jesus
Uninvited guest	**Host/Pharisee**	**Guest of honour** **Takes place at table**

• comes to attend Jesus
• waits; weeps;
• tears fall on feet;
  wipes them with hair;
• covers feet with kisses;
• anoints them with ointment
		• Jesus allows woman to do
		  what she has to do

	• When Simon sees this,
	  he talks to himself
	• **about Jesus** = If this man
	  were a prophet…
	• **about the woman** = Bad name
	  of the one that touches Jesus
		• Ministers to Simon
		• "I have something to say to
		  you, Simon"
		• Tries fiction/parable

		Jesus confronts his host: "Simon, do you see this woman?" He tries truth telling by comparing behaviour of Simon and the woman. Jesus questions Simon about his attitude, not the woman about her behaviour.
• pours out tears (water) • covers feet with kisses • anoints feet with ointment	• no water • no kiss • no anointing	
She is forgiven her "many sins" therefore shown great love Her faith has saved her; goes in peace	The man who is forgiven little shows little love	Jesus sees Simon as a man with no outreach; Jesus sees the woman as one who shows great love

See Mark 14:9

*"Truly I tell you, wherever the good news is proclaimed in the whole world, this story will be
proclaimed in memory of her."*

27 THE TRANSFIGURATION

1) Transfiguration as a theme

Telling stories of transfiguration from literature and life, reflecting on the profound hope of transformation at the heart of the human story.

- A story from the tradition of legend/fairytale
- A story from life: one woman's experience
- A story from modern literature

At the heart of each story there is a revelation: *something* that wasn't clear before now shows through, and that something is induced by a sign of graciousness/love. Nothing is what it seemed before. As in the stories, so in the Gospel: there is bread that is not just bread; there is wine that is not just wine; there is littleness that is not just littleness; there is a prophet who is not just a prophet. There is always more than meets the eye.

2) Hypotheses

The story of the transfiguration in the Gospels is a very complex one, and there are currently four hypotheses claiming our critical attention.

i)   It is a historical event in the Galilean ministry of Jesus, *a factual experience in which Jesus' divinity was manifested* to three privileged disciples. This view presupposes a fifth-century view of Jesus' divinity read back into the Gospel. It also makes it difficult to explain Peter's later denial of Jesus and the disciples' defection.

ii) It is a *vision experience* of Peter and the disciples like those experienced by Joan of Arc and other religious luminaries. This view psychologises the entire account.

iii) It is *an appearance of the risen Jesus* retrojected into the Galilean ministry, a view supported by the author of 2 Peter 1:16-18 who appears to understand the transfiguration as a resurrection story. This view fails to account for the other elements in the story: the presence of Moses and Elijah, the cloud, and the voice from heaven.

iv) It is *a symbolic story* that depicts Jesus as the Son of Man in the glory of the parousia. This view focuses on the literary text without touching the question of the historical problem.

Critical opinions vary so dramatically that the Jesuit biblical scholar J. Fitzmyer offers the cautious conclusion:

> *"Given the diversity of the way in which the incident is reported, no real historical judgement can be made about it; to write it all off as mythical is likewise to go beyond the evidence. Just what sort of an incident it was in the ministry of Jesus — to which it is clearly related — is impossible to say."* (The Gospel according to Luke, *1-9, p. 796*)

3) An example of Luke's architecture

There are some notable points of contact between Luke's account of the transfiguration and his story of the ascension. (See diagram) Note how Luke's resurrection account includes some of these elements: some women (followers of Jesus) go to the tomb; in a state of bewilderment and fear, they see two men, who are dressed in *dazzling clothes;* the two men are crucial in the narrative because the women cannot make

Shown on the left is Mount Tabor, which Christian tradition has located as the scene of the transfiguration. Situated in the north-west corner of the Jezreel Valley, Mount Tabor rises steeply and majestically to a height of 1,938 ft above the plain below. An outstanding landmark, it can be seen from great distances. Its visual splendour, in the shape of a perfect breast, and its aura of the sacred have always evoked admiration and wonder: "Tabor and Hermon rejoice in your name" (Ps 89:12).

The transfiguration	The ascension
• Jesus and disciples go up mountain (Lk 9:28)	• Jesus and disciples go up Mt. of Olives
• Mention of dazzling white clothes (9:29)	• Mention of white robes (Acts 1:10)
• Appearance of two men (9:30)	• Appearance of two men (1:10)
• These men interpret what is happening: Jesus' going up to Jerusalem (9:31)	• These men interpret what is happening: Jesus' going up to heaven (1:11)
• A cloud overshadows them (9:34)	• A cloud takes him from sight (1:9)

sense of their new experience. The two men *interpret the significance of the event:* "He is not here; he has risen."

4) The structure of the transfiguration
There are three accounts of the transfiguration: Mark 9:2-10; Luke 9:28-36; Matthew 17:1-9. The Fourth Gospel has no narrative of the incident. In Mark and Matthew the stress is on the disciples: "in their presence he was transfigured". The disciples are clearly in the foreground of the story, "Elijah appeared *to them* with Moses". In Luke the disciples are present, but in the background. The first part of Luke's story focuses on *Jesus* and that clue

suggests it is an older version than the accounts that concentrate on the *meaning of Jesus* for the disciples, in Mark and Matthew.

simple element
• Jesus goes up a mountain to pray accompanied by three disciples.
• While he prays, he changes. Something happens to him.

wonderful element
• Moses and Elijah appear and speak to Jesus: his *exodos* will be accomplished in Jerusalem.
• Voice speaks from cloud: "This is my Son, the Chosen One. Listen to him."

5) The context of the story

a) Luke tells us that Jesus goes up the mountain to pray. Jesus' purpose is to pray, not to manifest himself to the disciples. The prayer of Jesus follows on from the questions of his identity, the first prophecy of the passion, and sayings about discipleship (9:18-27). After his prayer experience, Jesus sets his face towards Jerusalem (9:51). Whatever the transfiguration does for the disciples, *Jesus' prayer experience enables him to face the city of his destiny.* In Luke that journey is the outcome of his prayer.

b) By this time in the Gospel narratve, there is mounting hostility towards Jesus. This opposition must have posed a problem for the historical Jesus. If the religious leaders are seeking his death, how can Jesus be expected to fulfil his mission from God? How can he reconcile the likelihood of his death with God's control of history?

• *Tension: awareness of mission versus likelihood of death*

c) There is also a question of whether, in this climate of religious opposition, anyone can believe Jesus' unique relationship with God, the one he calls "Abba". Most of Jesus' contemporaries think he is someone else – John the Baptist, Elijah, or one of the great prophets.

• *Tension: Jesus' relationship with "Abba" versus who people say he is*

6) An interpretation of the story

a) As in the baptism story, the wonderful element serves to interpret the meaning of the prayer experience – in this case, by illustrating the answer to Jesus' prayer.

b) Moses and Elijah, both of whom received revelations while praying on top of Mt Sinai (Horeb) appear and speak of Jesus' *journey to*

death as an accomplishment in Jerusalem. If death/accomplishment is given as an answer to Jesus' prayer, what is the question? Remember that the two disciples of Emmaus could not combine two ideas: the violent death of Jesus and the hope of Israel. For them, as for most people, death destroys hope. In the transfiguration we are told that Jesus' death will not be in tension with his mission: the contrary is true, *his death will be his mission.*

c) If the answer to Jesus' prayer is the proclamation, "This is my Son, the Chosen One", what is the question? Everyone's guesses about Jesus' identity are far from the mark; and Peter's incomplete confession of Jesus as Messiah is corrected by Jesus' reference to how the Son of Man must suffer (Lk 9:22; see Mk 8:33). No one can hold securely to his or her identity without the support of significant others. Recognition of who we are is an essential part of identity formation. In Jesus' prayer experience there is the affirmation of who Jesus is, which is a clear corrective to Peter's suggestion for a building programme. Without loading the declaration with the weight of later Christology, it is still an affirmation of Jesus' sonship and election as the Chosen One.

d) When the two Old Testament figures have disappeared, Luke notes, "Jesus was found alone." The focus is on the person of Jesus. He alone, not the great figures from the Old Testament, stands between heaven and earth. He alone will face the consequences of the revelation: the Chosen One will now take the road to Jerusalem in the declared love of his Father. The transfiguration is a confirmation of Jesus' *identity* and *direction*.

7) Against claiming too much

When they all come down from the mountain, Jesus speaks his second prophecy of the passion and the consequences of the mountain revelation are underlined. Luke says of the disciples: ***"They did not understand when he said this; it was hidden from them so they should not see the meaning of it, and they were afraid to ask him what he had just said"*** (9:45).

Luke discounts an interpretation that claims that the transfiguration was a manifestation to the disciples of Jesus' secret identity and purpose. The revelation to the disciples of who Jesus is will happen only after the resurrection, when the disciples are "clothed with the power from on high" (24:49).

8) Transfiguration in life

Transfiguration is not a solitary event in the Gospel, but one that happens over and over again. Throughout his public ministry, Jesus transfigures many people – the broken, the wounded, and the wayward. He calls to the deepest part of people; he sees in the afflicted more than others see: "Simon, do you see this woman?" Jesus' whole healing ministry is transfiguring the broken through the power of God's love. The power that transfigured Jesus is the same power that works through him in transforming others.

The experience of transfiguration can be interpreted as one where Jesus grows closer to who he really is. And we all grow closer to who we really are when we hear our name called in love. When that happens we become radiant and we are better enabled to face the future – whatever it holds. We can better understand the transfiguration when we ask: what would it take to transfigure us? Who could transfigure us? Who calls our name in love? Whose name do we call in love? If it is true that we have within us the capacity to disfigure people, it is equally true that we have within us the capacity to transfigure others.

Mosaic in the Basilica of the Transfiguration, Mt Tabor, Galilee

FURTHER READING

R. Marshal,	*The Transfiguration of Jesus* (London: DLT, 1994)
J. Fitzmyer,	*The Gospel according to Luke, 1-9* pp. 791-804
F. Wright Beare,	*The Gospel according to Matthew* pp. 360-365
R.H. Stein,	"Is the Transfiguration a misplaced resurrection account?" *Journal of Biblical Literature* 95 (1976) pp. 79-96
J. Moltmann,	"The Transformation of Life" in *The Power of the Powerless* (London: SCM, 1983) pp. 64-70
D. McBride,	Reflections on the Transfiguration in *Seasons of the Word* pp. 76-81

REFLECTION: FAITH HEALING
BY PHILIP LARKIN

Slowly the women file to where he stands
Upright in rimless glasses, silver hair,
Dark suit, white collar. Stewards tirelessly
Persuade them onwards to his voice and hands,
Within whose warm spring rain of loving care
Each dwells some twenty seconds. Now, dear child,
What's wrong, the deep American voice demands,
And, scarcely pausing, goes into a prayer
Directing God about this eye, that knee.
Their heads are clasped abruptly; then, exiled

Like losing thoughts, they go in silence; some
Sheepishly stray, not back into their lives
Just yet; but some stay stiff, twitching and loud
With deep hoarse tears, as if a kind of dumb
And idiot child within them still survives

To re-awake at kindness, thinking a voice
At last calls them alone, that hands have come
To lift and lighten; and such joy arrives
Their thick tongues blort, their eyes squeeze grief, a crowd
Of huge unheard answers jam and rejoice –

What's wrong! Moustached in flowered frocks they shake:
By now, all's wrong. In everyone there sleeps
A sense of life lived according to love -
To some it means the difference they could make
By loving others, but across most it sweeps
As all they might have done had they been loved.
That nothing cures. An immense slackening ache,
As when, thawing, the rigid landscape weeps,
Spreads slowly through them – that, and the voice above
Saying Dear child, and all time has disproved.

Philip Larkin, The Whitsun Weddings *(London: Faber & Faber, 1963) p.15*

SUFFERING, PRAYER & PASSION

1) Paying attention to pain or avoiding all pain

"Merciful heaven!
What, man! Ne'er pull your hat upon your brows;
Give sorrow words; the grief that does not speak
Whispers the o'erfraught heart and bids it break."

(Shakespeare Macbeth, *IV, iii, 208*)

"As for me, Lord, I call unto you for help:
In the morning my prayer comes before you.
Lord, why do you reject me?
Why do you hide your face?

Wretched, close to death from my youth,
I have borne your trials; I am numb.
Your fury has swept down upon me;
Your terrors have utterly destroyed me…

Friend and neighbour you have taken away:
My one companion is darkness."

(Ps 88: 13-18)

"Apathy is a form of the inability to suffer. It is understood as a social condition in which people are so dominated by the goal of avoiding the suffering that it becomes a goal to avoid human relationships and contacts altogether… The desire to remain free from suffering, the retreat into apathy, can be a kind of fear of contact. One doesn't want to be touched, infected, defiled, drawn in. One remains aloof to the greatest possible extent, concerns himself with his own affairs, isolates himself to the point of dull-wittedness."

(D. Soelle, Suffering, *pp. 36, 39*)

2) The biblical tradition: finding a language for pain

The biblical prayer of lamentation expresses deep mourning in the face of a profound loss: it is the human response to death and dying in the midst of life. Loss is one of the most common occurrences in the calendar of human experience: lamentation gives that loss expression; it allows the individual or the community to express that loss, to act it out, to shout it to the heavens. To lament is to give vent to the sense of defeat and deprivation, rather than hoard the pain or nurse it; it is to go public on loss in the hope that the lamentation will change the experience, in the hope that the empty place in the heart will be filled with consolation and support.

In Hebrew, *kinah*, the dirge, expresses the loss that is keenly felt. That is usually accompanied by weeping: so Abraham grieves at the death of Sarah (Gen 23:2); Joseph weeps at the death of his father (Gen 50:1); David laments the death of Saul and Jonathan (2 Sam 1:17-27); the mothers wail at the loss of their murdered infants (Mt 2:18); Jesus is moved to tears at the death of Lazarus (Jn 11:35) and weeps at the thought of the coming destruction of Jerusalem (Lk 19:41).

The mourning customs of Israel also included wailing, groaning, beating the breast, tearing hair, rending clothes, and fasting. Professional mourners were hired – not to manipulate

In Edvard Munch's painting,
The Scream, *a person stands on a bridge, holding his head between his hands, his eyes open in fear, his mouth open in screaming. The painter catches a real incident that he wrote about in his diary. "I was walking along the street with two friends – the sun was going down – I felt a touch of melancholy. Suddenly the colour of the sky changed to blood-red. I stopped walking and leaned against a fence feeling tired to death. I saw the flaming clouds like bloodstained swords... the blue-black fjord and the city... my friends went on walking... I stood there trembling with fear, and I felt how a long unending scream was going through the whole of nature."*

For Munch, art was not the expression of the perceived world, but the articulation of the subjective, inner world of feeling. Munch used the story of his own painful childhood (at the age of 5 he lost his mother, and a few years later his sister) and shaped what his inner eye saw in flowing forms of simple design. Many people were affronted at his lack of good taste, for making public what should have been kept private – personal loss and fear and an overwhelming sense of wretchedness. In **The Scream** *(1893) the Norwegian painter makes international currency out of what is essentially a private pain. An individual's scream is the vehicle that liberates from the captivity of kept anguish.*

people's feelings, but to help the real mourners find some expression for their grief. Mourning was also a reaction to the downfall of nations: Jeremiah tells the people to mourn their lost relationship with God (Jer 9:17-22), just as he bemoans the day he was born (Jer 20:7-18).

The prayers of lamentation form the largest category of the psalms. They are cries from the heart, shouts of suffering, groans of anguish, screams for help, protests against what is happening. They are written on a bed of pain in the hope that God or someone will listen and intervene.

3) Lamentation and change

Phase One

The biblical tradition of lamentation tries to free people from remaining mute and isolated in their pain. Extreme suffering can render people blind and deaf to the outside world; it can turn people in on themselves, reducing them to vegetation. That kind of suffering excludes change and learning.

People can become so dominated by the situation that their only feeling is powerlessness. They suffer in silence. This, like all suffering, demands respect. As Saint-Exupéry said, "It is such a secret place, the land of tears."

Phase One	Phase Two	Phase Three
mute	lamenting	changing
speechless	aware	organising
isolated	expressing	sharing
dominated by situation	suffering from situation	shaping the situation
powerlessness	struggle	acceptance/change of structures

Phase Two

The first step out of speechless isolation is to find a language of pain, of description, of protest. This phase refuses to stay with a "humility" that is indistinguishable from pessimism: active behaviour replaces reactive submission. Phase Two is essential for moving forward to liberation/acceptance. It is a bridge between isolation and community, between a powerless silence and commitment to change:

> "Speak yourself on behalf of the dumb on behalf of all the unwanted; speak yourself, pronounce a just verdict, uphold the rights of the poor and needy."
> (Prov 31:8-9)

Phase Three

The purpose of the above progress is not just self-expression: it is taking responsibility for the suffering that can be changed; it is a refusal to remain apathetic. If people refuse to speak about their suffering, they will be destroyed by it. To elect speechlessness is death; it is to volunteer for hell, the place where there is no change. If people believe God is like the idols "with eyes that never see, ears that never hear, hands that never touch", they will "end up like them" (Ps 115). We are doomed or liberated to repeat our own image of God.

Through awareness, people come to knowledge of the suffering they can change and the suffering that has to be accepted. There is much avoidable suffering that is permitted to thrive through apathy. But life also teaches of a suffering that cannot be avoided. Jesus' criticism of how the religious authorities are damaging people is an example of the kind of imposed suffering Jesus sees as avoidable. On the other hand, the cross of Jesus stands as recognition of the kind of suffering that has to be taken on. This is not passive toleration of suffering; it is an affirmation that there is such a reality as meaningful suffering, suffering as passion.

This is the story of Gethsemane and the passion. It is the Christian story *ex memoria passionis*, a story proclaimed out of the dangerous memory of suffering.

4) **The three phases exemplified in Luke 18:36-43 and Gethsemane**
On the final stage of his journey to death, Jesus heals the blind man who screams for help. By comparison the crowd wants the blind man to stay quiet. You can see how the story depicts the three phases of the biblical tradition; how Jesus will repeat those stages in his prayer in Gethsemane.

FURTHER READING

D. McBride,	"Towards a spirituality of dying and death" in *Studies in Formative Spirituality* (1981) Vol. 2 No. 2 pp. 179-188
L. Dunlop,	*Patterns of Prayer in the Psalms* (New York: Seabury, 1982) pp. 95-150
S. Mowinckel,	*The Psalms in Israel's Worship* (Oxford: Blackwell, 1967) Vol. 1 pp.139-224; Vol. 2 pp. 1-25
D. Soelle,	*Suffering* (Philadelphia: Fortress, 1975) pp. 61-86
C. Brown (Ed),	"Lament" in *Dictionary of New Testament Theology* (Exeter: Paternoster, 1976) Vol. 2 pp. 416-424

In memory of him: retelling the stories of Jesus

"It is often said, rightly, that Christianity is a historical religion. This means that the distinctive truth that the Christian religion believes and teaches can only be expressed and conveyed in the form of story.

"A great deal of ordinary conversation consists of the telling, hearing and exchanging of stories. Stories report events – particular things that have happened in this eventful world. In contrast statements convey general truths about the world itself and every thing or person that the world contains. So, for instance, 'there was a major earthquake in Japan last night' is a story, whereas 'Japan is very often affected by earthquakes' is a statement. Both stories and statements contain and convey information, but the effect of information conveyed by a story tends to be rather more powerful than that of information conveyed by a statement.

"The meaning of stories cannot be summarised in general statements and conveyed intact in a different verbal container. The story itself must be told or written and heard or read: only so can its meaning be fully received and understood. But its meaning is not, so to speak, written in stone: the impact and effect of the story will be different at different times and for different people."

(W.H. Vanstone, Fare Well in Christ (London: DLT, 1997) pp. 19, 20, 26)

1. Theology and storytelling may seem, at first glance, unlikely companions, yet there has been, in recent years, a rediscovery of the roots of theology in narrative (see reading list for a representative sample of works). If Christian theology naturally tends towards the analytical and faith towards dogmatic assertion in creeds, both can find renewal in a return to their roots in the imaginative storytelling of Jesus. Jesus did much of his theological thinking through storytelling and parable; he chose fiction as his popular method of communicating the breadth and the depth and the height of the kingdom of God.

2. In Western culture when we ask a question or seek for insight, we expect a direct answer or discussion; we don't expect someone to appeal to our imagination and tell us a story. And yet in Jesus' world, a story was an appropriate way to respond to enquiry and criticism. In the Gospels no one appears puzzled that Jesus tells stories, although many are confused or angry or delighted by the kind of stories that he tells. He rarely explains his stories, leaving them as a gift to be unwrapped by his listeners.

   Jesus comes, like the painting on the right, as the dancing story, inviting people to find their own rhythm in enigmatic tales and cryptic parables, challenging his listeners to uncover within themselves new ways of thinking.

3. The Gospel message as spoken proclamation reflected the personal, immediate form of communication Jesus used in his own

ministry: human speech in face-to-face encounter. The spoken word, more than the written, is directed to an actual person at the present moment – consequently, the hearer of a living voice is confronted more immediately than the reader of sentences. Direct speech, more than sacred writing or places or times or rituals, has characterised the movement of Christianity from its beginning in Jesus. As Wilder observed: "Jesus was a voice, not a penman, a herald not a scribe, a watchman with his call in the market-place and the Temple, and not a cry of alarm in the wilderness like John the Baptist. This deportment of Jesus is a sign…Jesus' word was for the present, the last hour" (A.N. Wilder, *Early Christian Rhetoric,* p.13).

4. Many of the parables Jesus told, as well as the stories about him, are so familiar to us that we can fail to hear them. J. R.R. Tolkien defined a good story as "familiar, but not too familiar; strange, but not too strange". If a story is too familiar, it can fail to purchase our interest; if it is too strange, it can leave us unmoved by its difference from our experience. The stories written in the Gospels have their own integrity and they are available for anyone to read. It may be worth the risk, however, to make Jesus' stories a little strange in the hope that we might hear them anew.

5. Jesus the storyteller was first a listener to stories; the teller was first a hearer. The stories told by the adult Jesus, together with the story of his life, are offered to us not only to be heard but also to be retold, not only to be analysed but also to be proclaimed.

Dancing story:
artist unknown

FURTHER READING

D. McBride,	*Impressions of Jesus*
J. Shea,	*An Experience Named Spirit,* pp. 88-141
S. McFague,	*Metaphorical Theology* (London: SCM, 1983)
M. Goldberg,	*Theology and Narrative* (Nashville: Abingdon, 1982)
R. Alter,	*The Art of Biblical Narrative* (London: Allen & Unwin, 1981)
J. Licht,	*Storytelling in the Bible* (Jerusalem: Magnes, 1978)
A.N. Wilder,	*Early Christian Rhetoric: the Language of the Gospel* (Cambridge: Harvard University Press, 1976)

REFLECTION: A LAST WORD
HABAKKUK 2:2-3

And the Lord answered me:

"Write the vision down,
inscribe it on tablets
to be easily read.
For still the vision
awaits its time.

It is eager for its own fulfilment;
it does not deceive.

If it comes slowly, wait,
for come it will,
without fail."

PICTURE CREDITS

THE FOLLOWING LECTURES OF FATHER DENIS MCBRIDE ARE AVAILABLE ON CD AND CASSETTE TAPES

Volume One — The beginning of the Gospels
1. Our first images of Jesus; first images of Mark and frame of Gospel
2. First Images of Matthew and frame of Gospel
3. Matthew concluded; first images of Luke and frame of Gospel
4. Luke concluded; first images of John and frame of Gospel

Volume Two — Leadership and discipleship
1. Stories of interaction in ministry; leadership in Gospels 1
2. Leadership 2; our identity, direction and outlook
3. The beginnings of discipleship in Mark and Luke
4. The beginnings of discipleship in John; fascination and discipleship

Volume Three — The Passion and Resurrection
1. Introducing the Passion; the city of Jerusalem
2. Separation and flight in Gethsemane
3. The language of the Passion: things happen to Jesus
4. Introducing the resurrection
5. The Emmaus narrative
6. The end of the Luke's Gospel: no man's land

Volume Four — The Formation of the Gospels
1. The beginning of the church 1: community of memory and Spirit
2. The beginning of the church 2
3. Formation of the Gospels
4. The bringing the past up to date

Volume Five — Jesus and John the Baptist
1. The beginning of the Jesus story with John the Baptist
2. John and Jesus in Mark and Matthew
3. John and Jesus in Luke and John
4. Similarities and differences

Volume Six — Mission and table fellowship
1. Jesus' mission: moving away from sacred space
2. Jesus' table-fellowship
3. At the house of Simon the Pharisee 1
4. At the house of Simon the Pharisee 2

Volume Seven — The road to Transformation
1. The Transfiguration 1
2. The Transfiguration 2

Further details and information can be found at www.ShineOnline.net. Alternatively, please ring the sales office for a brochure and further details +44 (0)1420 88222